Teach Yourself VISUALLY
Guitar

Second Edition

Teach Yourself VISUALLY™

Guitar

Second Edition

by Charles Kim

WILEY

John Wiley & Sons, Inc.

Credits

Acquisitions Editor
Pam Mourouzis

Project Editor
Suzanne Snyder

Technical Editor
Geoff Dolce

Editorial Manager
Christina Stambaugh

Vice President and Publisher
Cindy Kitchel

Vice President and Executive Publisher
Kathy Nebenhaus

Interior Design
Kathie Rickard
Elizabeth Brooks

Photography
Matt Bowen

Graphics and Production Specialists
Joyce Haughey
Sennett Vaughan Johnson
Brent Savage

Teach Yourself VISUALLY™ *Guitar,* **2nd Edition**

Copyright © 2012 by John Wiley & Sons, Inc., Hoboken, New Jersey. All rights reserved.

Published by John Wiley & Sons, Inc., Hoboken, New Jersey
Published simultaneously in Canada

For general information on our other products and services or to obtain technical support, please contact our Customer Care Department within the U.S. at (877) 762-2974, outside the U.S. at (317) 572-3993 or fax (317) 572-4002.

Wiley also publishes its books in a variety of electronic formats and by print-on-demand. Not all content that is available in standard print versions of this book may appear or be packaged in all book formats. If you have purchased a version of this book that did not include media that is referenced by or accompanies a standard print version, you may request this media by visiting booksupport.wiley.com. For more information about Wiley products, visit us at www.wiley.com.

Library of Congress Control Number: 2011943434
ISBN: 978-1-118-13334-7 (pbk)
ISBN: 978-1-118-20627-0 (ebk)
ISBN: 978-1-118-20628-7 (ebk)
ISBN: 978-1-118-21713-9 (ebk)

Printed in the United States of America

10 9 8 7 6 5 4 3 2 1

Book production by John Wiley & Sons, Inc., Composition Services

About the Author

Charles Kim (Chicago, IL) plays guitar, electric and upright bass, pedal steel, banjo, violin, alto saxophone, piano, keyboards, and drums. He teaches guitar, bass, songwriting, recording, and music theory at Chicago's renowned Old Town School of Folk Music. A multifaceted musician, producer, and composer featured on numerous albums, Kim is also a composer and sound designer for film, TV, dance, and theatre companies.  His scores have been commissioned and featured by the Royal Academy of Art, Showtime, and the History Channel.

Acknowledgments

I would like to sincerely thank my editors Pam Mourouzis and Suzanne Snyder for giving me the opportunity to write this book. Audrey Cho was kind enough to take my photo. I'd also like to thank my family, friends, bandmates, and the Old Town School of Folk Music, who supported me to grow as a musician. This book is dedicated to my mother, Hai Ja Kim, who was my first music teacher.

Special Thanks...

To the following companies for granting us permission to show photos of their equipment:

- Reno's Music
- Sweetwater

Table of Contents

Table of Contents

CHAPTER 1

Learning
to Play

You've chosen to start off on a musical adventure: playing the guitar.

Let's take a look at some of the facets of the instrument and the dif-

ferent musical options it offers. I'll also show you how to create a

practice plan and pursue your guitar playing into the future.

Compared to other instruments, the guitar is a relatively easy instrument to learn. You can play it from the first day, using a few simple chords. You'll be playing in just a few pages!

START PLAYING TODAY

Violin and trumpet students have to practice diligently for years to play a major scale with a warm tone in tune. While the guitar will eventually make its intricacies known to you, you can learn the first three chords (see Chapter 6) and a simple strumming pattern (see Chapter 9) on your first day. The frets, which divide the string length, do the job of keeping you in tune, and you'll play simple rhythms until you develop more coordination. Although you'll eventually want to reach higher levels of proficiency, you can start creating music right away!

SET GOALS FOR YOURSELF

The trick to teaching yourself anything is to practice on a steady schedule and to set realistic goals. Give yourself time to learn, and don't get discouraged if things don't come to you immediately.

People often become their own worst enemies when learning a musical instrument because they set unrealistic goals. Remember that mastering an instrument is a learning process that is both mental and physical. You understand what you have to do, but training your hands takes time. Allow your body to develop muscle strength and memory, which are slower to develop in an adult. You will eventually develop those skills, so don't lose patience!

PRACTICE THE RIGHT WAY

Develop a reasonable but steady practice regimen. Try to practice every day, if only for 15 or 20 minutes. If you can't practice every day, try not to put your guitar away for several days in a row. Make sure you're playing at least every other day. Leave the guitar next to the TV or somewhere else where you'll see it often, and let your hands get used to the instrument in your spare time.

Starting and stopping your guitar playing will only make the process more discouraging. You will probably progress more quickly than you realize or give yourself credit for. Be prepared to work through the rough spots. Your efforts eventually will be rewarded!

Keep the learning experience fun by playing songs you love. Doing so will take the "work" element out of practicing, and you'll master the skills you need before you know it!

Continue Your Guitar Education

Now that you've started your musical journey with the guitar, you'll want to find ways to pursue your playing. Here are some options to consider as you use this book as a reference.

WORK WITH A PRIVATE TEACHER

After you've worked on some of the basics, you might seek the guidance of a private instructor. You can work with a teacher on individual playing issues and specialize in different types of music.

Nothing can replace the inspiration and clarity that come from working with a professional musician. Use this book as a resource while your teacher helps you focus on specific issues. He or she can design a special program of songs and exercises to take your playing to the next level of proficiency.

LEARN FROM OTHER GUITARISTS

Part of the beauty of music is the interaction and sharing you experience when playing with others. Learn from your friends as you use your guitar as an outlet for musical communication. Continue the learning experience by playing with other musicians who are slightly more experienced than you are. You'll gain guidance and inspiration, as well as ideas about what to pursue in your independent studies or with your instructor.

Also play with friends who are beginning guitarists like you. Realize that some of your friends might learn certain things faster than you; don't worry about it or compare yourself negatively to them. Every guitarist finds certain tasks easier than others. Your friend may find it easy to play barre chords, but find it difficult to play finger-style guitar as well as you do. Everyone's development differs from skill to skill.

> **TIP**
>
> Make sure you're clear on what your teacher expects from you in terms of both short-term and long-term development. That way, you will know how to realistically gauge your progress and spare yourself unnecessary frustration.

Remember to set realistic goals for yourself. Don't set your standards so high that if you don't meet them, you get discouraged and give up. Muscle strength and muscle memory don't develop overnight, but with consistent practice you will develop them eventually.

PRACTICE, PRACTICE, PRACTICE!

Practice is most effective when it is regular and consistent. Practicing for half an hour a day is better than cramming in a four-hour session once a week. Muscles and reflexes need a regimen to stay sharp. If you know you won't be able to practice every day, then try to play every other day. If you're taking lessons, try to practice a little right after you meet with your instructor. Doing so provides a great chance to ingrain what you have learned while it is fresh in your mind.

WORK ON DIFFERENT SKILLS

As you continue to learn new skills, including different fretting techniques, lead guitar, and different rhythmic approaches, you may find that certain ones are harder to master than others. Don't let work in one area stop you from working on skills in other areas. For example, don't feel that you have to master barre chords before you experiment with lead guitar. You may find that you have a knack for vibrato and string bending, but your index finger muscles may need to develop some strength before you can perform these skills competently.

Finally, don't forget to have fun! Don't let technical goals obscure the reason you picked up the guitar in the first place.

CHAPTER 2

Parts of the Guitar

All guitars have similar essential features. Before you start playing, let's take a look at the different parts of the electric and the acoustic guitar.

Let's get acquainted with the most common parts of the acoustic guitar.

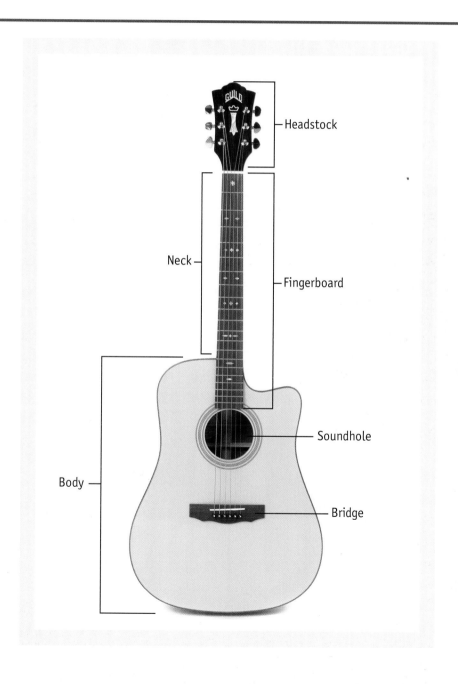

Headstock

Neck

Fingerboard

Body

Soundhole

Bridge

Parts of the Electric Guitar

ow let's look at the parts of the electric guitar. Some of them are similar to the acoustic guitar, while other components—especially those involving electronics—are different.

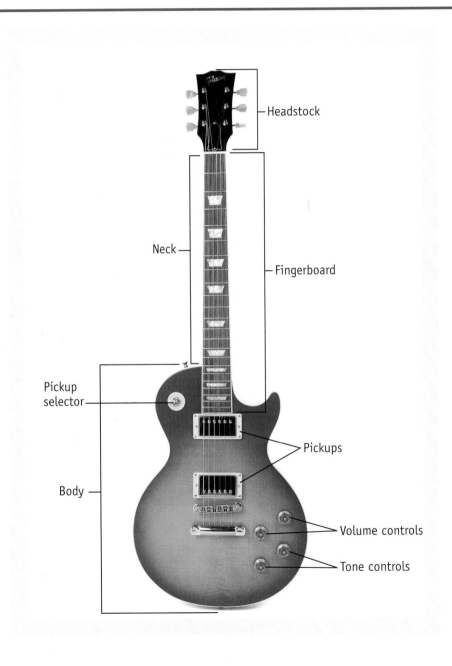

- Headstock
- Neck
- Fingerboard
- Pickup selector
- Body
- Pickups
- Volume controls
- Tone controls

Now let's look at the parts of both acoustic and electric guitars in more detail, starting with the top of the instrument—the headstock—which contains the tuners.

HEADSTOCK

The headstock is where the strings end at the tuning pegs.

TUNING PEGS

The tuning pegs or tuners tighten or loosen the tension of the strings, thus raising or lowering the pitch. You adjust the tuning pegs to keep the guitar in tune. Most acoustic guitars, steel-string and nylon, and some electric guitars have three tuners on the top and three on the bottom of the headstock.

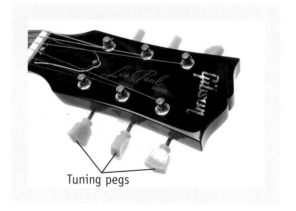

Tuning pegs

Some electric guitars have their tuners all along the top, six in a row, as shown here.

Neck

The neck is where you place your fretting hand. If you are a right-handed player, your fretting hand is your left hand; if you're left-handed, it is your right hand. The fretting hand's fingers press on top of the strings, while the thumb provides support on the back of the neck.

FINGERBOARD

The fingerboard is the playing surface of the neck, which is divided by the guitar's frets and stretches down to the body of the guitar.

Fingerboard

MARKERS

The markers enable you to find a specific fret quickly. Some are simple dots; other guitars have ornate inlays. Most manufacturers of steel-string and electric guitars place markers at the 3rd, 5th, 7th, 9th, 12th, and 15th frets.

Markers

SIDE MARKERS

Many guitars have side markers in addition to finger-board markers, as shown here. Classical and other nylon-string guitars usually have markers only on the side of the neck, and not on the fingerboard itself.

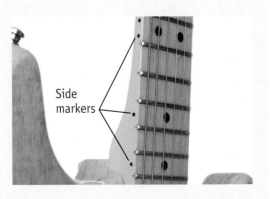

Side markers

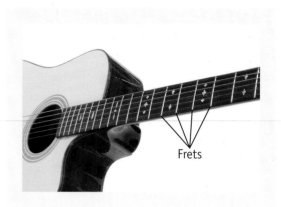

NUT

The nut stops the vibration on one side of the string. (The bridge works on the other side.) Nuts can be made of bone, plastic, brass, or other compound material.

FRETS

The frets are thin strips that run perpendicular to the strings. You place your fingers on the strings behind the frets, which changes the pitch by shortening the strings.

TRUSS ROD

Because of string tension and how wood bends with changes in temperature and humidity, many guitars have a truss rod—a metal bar that helps straighten or curve the neck angle. You can find it at the top or the base of the neck. Nylon-string guitars do not have a truss rod.

HEEL

The heel is where the back of the neck joins the body of the guitar. It can be plain or elaborate, depending on the style of the guitar.

Body

The body of the guitar houses the rest of its components. On acoustic and hollow or semi-hollow electric guitars, the body shape, composition, and wood type heavily influence the guitar's sound. On electric guitars with solid bodies, the body plays a slightly less important role.

The steel-string guitar body usually has a soundhole, which allows the guitar to resonate. The bridge holds the strings in place using bridge pins.

Solid-body guitars are the most common electric guitars sold today. Some, like the Gibson SG, the Fender Telecaster, and the Les Paul (pictured at right), have bodies that are sculpted out of solid wood.

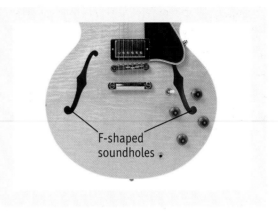

ROUND SOUNDHOLE

The soundhole enables the sound of the guitar to breathe and project. Some guitars have round or oval soundholes.

F-SHAPED SOUNDHOLES

Early models, especially hollow and semi-hollow guitars, have F-shaped soundholes similar to those found on a violin or cello.

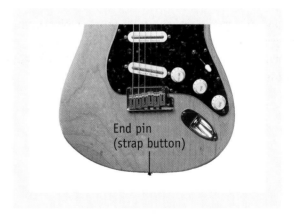

PICK GUARD

The pick guard's function is to ensure that pick strokes don't scratch the surface of the wood.

END PIN

There is usually a button at the end of the guitar around which you can attach a strap. For more on playing with a strap, see Chapter 4.

The bridge anchors the strings to the body of the guitar. There are a variety of bridge styles depending on the type of guitar.

Bridge pin

STEEL-STRING BRIDGE

On a steel-string guitar, the strings are fastened by bridge pins to a wooden bridge. The tension of the strings keeps the pins fastened.

TELECASTER BRIDGE

In the Fender Telecaster, the strings pass through the body and a metal bridge, which allows the strings to ring longer.

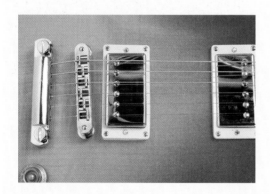

TUNE-O-MATIC BRIDGE

Frequently found on Gibson Les Pauls and SGs, the Tune-o-matic Bridge has a tailpiece where the strings end and a set of six adjustable saddles that can be fine-tuned for intonation.

STRATOCASTER BRIDGE

Some guitar bridges move by depressing a vibrato bar. These bridges are suspended between springs with adjustable tension and a set of screws that act as a fulcrum.

Depending on the type of guitar you're playing, you will use either nylon or steel strings.

STEEL STRINGS

Steel strings are used on acoustic and electric guitars for country, rock, pop, blues, and slide playing. They have a brighter sound than nylon strings, and have more tension.

The two highest-pitched strings (B and High E) usually are plain steel, while the others are wrapped. The steel itself can be made of phosphor bronze, nickel, or stainless steel.

NYLON STRINGS

Nylon strings are used in classical, flamenco, and certain folk guitars. These strings were traditionally made from animal gut. They have a warmer and darker sound than steel strings. Nylon strings also feel softer to the touch and need less tension to achieve their pitch. The three highest-pitched strings (G, B, and High E) usually are plain nylon, while the Low E, A, and D strings are wrapped with another winding of nylon.

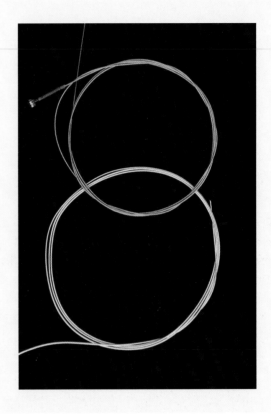

Electric guitars are played in the same way as acoustic guitars, but they can sound radically different. Their electronic controls allow you to manipulate tonal variety and sound.

Pickups

The pickups are the microphonic elements that transfer the sound of the strings to the electronic output in an electric guitar. The most common types are the single-coil pickup and the humbucker pickup.

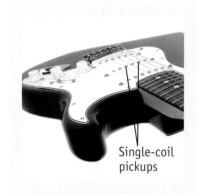

Single-coil pickups

Humbucker pickups

Pickup selector

SINGLE-COIL PICKUP

The single-coil pickup has a clear, bright sound.

HUMBUCKER PICKUP

The humbucker pickup is actually two single coils wrapped together with wire to combat electric noise and buzzing. In relation to the single-coil pickup, the humbucker pickup has a deeper, darker sound.

SELECTOR SWITCH

The closer the pickup is to the bridge, the more treble the pickup has. A selector switch is used to select which pickup or combination of pickups is active.

Volume Controls

SINGLE VOLUME CONTROL

The volume control regulates how loud or soft the guitar is. Some guitars, like the Telecaster, have one volume control.

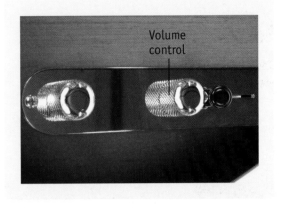

Volume
control

LES PAUL VOLUME CONTROLS

Other guitars, like the Les Paul, have volume controls that control each pickup individually.

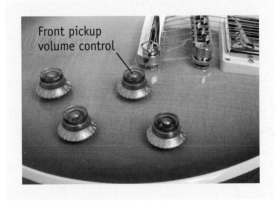

Front pickup
volume control

Tone Controls and Output Jack

The tone controls determine how much treble is removed from a pickup's sound, making the guitar sound darker.

Tone control

Some guitars, like the Telecaster, have one tone control. Others, like the Les Paul and the Gibson ES-335 (shown here), have a tone control that controls each pickup individually.

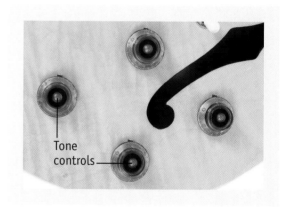

Tone controls

One end of the patch cord is plugged in the output jack of the guitar, and the other end is plugged in the amplifier to complete the signal path for the guitar's sound.

TIP

Be careful with a loose jack. Twisting a cable in a loose jack could cause internal wires to twist and eventually break.

Output jack

CHAPTER 3

Tuning the Guitar

Before you start playing, you need to learn how to get your guitar in tune. In this chapter, you'll learn how to tune both with an electronic tuner and with your ears, using a method called relative tuning.

Before you start playing, make sure your guitar is in tune so that all the chords sound musically correct. The open strings need to be tuned to the notes E, A, D, G, B, and E, in the order of fattest string to thinnest. The Low E (6th), or fattest, string is closest to your head as you hold the guitar. The High E (1st), or thinnest, string is closest to your feet.

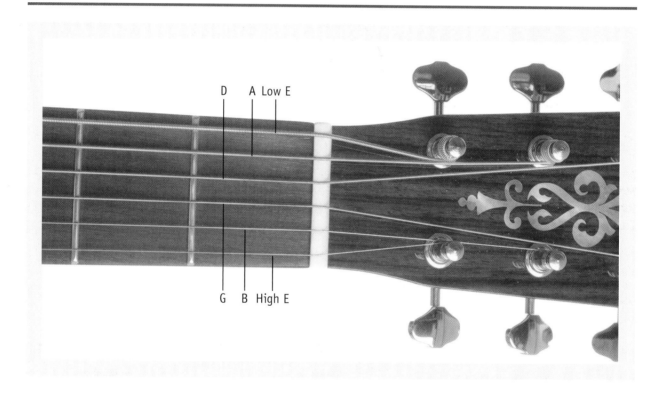

We'll start by tuning with an electronic tuner so you can begin playing as soon as possible. Here you'll learn how the different strings are tuned and the scale you need to be aware of while you're tuning.

If you're tuning an electric guitar, you plug one end of a ¼-inch cable into the output jack of your guitar and the other end into the jack of the tuner. Make sure that the volume control on your guitar is all the way up, and tune as if you were tuning an acoustic guitar.

Use a Chromatic Tuner and the Chromatic Scale

Purchase a small electronic chromatic tuner to tune your guitar, as opposed to just a guitar or bass tuner. This way, even if a string is tuned to the wrong note, you can figure out which way you need to tune to correct the problem. Note that the term *tuner* in this context is different from the physical tuners (tuning pegs) on the guitar's neck that you turn to change a string's pitch (see Chapter 2).

A chromatic tuner tells you where the pitch of a string is on the chromatic scale. The chromatic scale is all the possible notes in the Western musical scale, as shown below.

C	C♯/D♭	D	D♯/E♭	E	F	F♯/G♭	G	G♯/A♭	A	A♯/B♭	B	C

←————— Lower Pitch Higher —————→

NOTE: The notes C♯ and D♭ are called *enharmonic notes* (discussed in greater detail in Chapter 13). They have the same pitch, but two potential names. The same applies for D♯ and E♭, F♯ and G♭, G♯ and A♭, and A♯ and B♭. Your tuner may list the notes only by their sharp names or their flat names.

TIP

If you notice that your guitar is constantly going out of tune, or that only certain chords will stay in tune, you need to change the strings (see Chapter 16). The strings have become fatigued and no longer have the strength to stay in tune.

Tune the Low E String

Let's tune the Low E (6th) string first.

1 Turn on the electronic tuner and place the guitar a couple of inches away from it.

NOTE: It's not unusual for the guitar to get way out of tune if it hasn't been played for a day or was bumped in transport.

You may want to cover the strings you aren't tuning so the tuner won't get confused by extra ringing strings. Use the palm of your picking hand, as shown here.

2 Pluck the Low E (6th) string and make sure that the string is in the vicinity of E, and not on a different chromatic pitch. Your electronic tuner has an indicator that shows you what general chromatic pitch you're on.

Chromatic pitch indicator

3 If the electronic tuner reads E, then you're ready to fine-tune your string.

If the electronic tuner reads C, C♯/D♭, D, or D♯/E♭, then your string is flat and the pitch is too low. Tighten the string by turning the tuning peg counterclockwise and raising the pitch until you reach the vicinity of E.

Turn counterclockwise if pitch is flat

If the electronic tuner reads F, F♯/G♭, or G, then your string is sharp and the pitch is too high. Loosen the string by turning the tuning peg clockwise until you reach the vicinity of E.

NOTE: On some guitars, the tuners are reversed so that the Low E tuning peg is on the bottom of the headstock. If you play one of these guitars, know that you'll need to turn the tuning pegs clockwise to raise the pitch and counterclockwise to lower it.

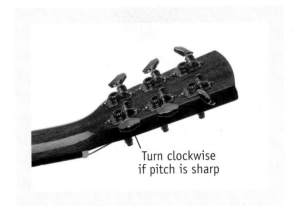

Turn clockwise
if pitch is sharp

FINE-TUNING

Once you've got the note of E in your chromatic pitch indicator window, you need to fine-tune it exactly to E. Look at the window with the digital "needle" indicator.

If the indicator is on the left side of the center line, then the note is flat. Turn the tuning peg counterclockwise to raise the pitch.

Tuner indicates flat

If the indicator is on the right side of the center line, then the note is sharp. Turn the tuning peg clockwise to lower the pitch.

Tuner indicates sharp

23

Once you've got both the E in the chromatic pitch indicator window and the needle in the center of the fine-tuning window, the string is in tune!

Tuner indicates E is in tune

The table below shows the tunings for the rest of the strings. If, for instance, the A (5th) string is flat, the indicator will point to A♭ or one of the other notes mentioned in the table's Flat column. If the A (5th) string is sharp, the indicator will point to A♯ or one of the other notes mentioned in the Sharp column. If the tuning for the A (5th) string is correct, the indicator will point to A, as shown in the "In Tune" column.

String	In Tune	Flat	Sharp
A (5th) string	A	F♯/G♭, G, G♯/A♭	A♯/B♭, B, C
D (4th) string	D	B, C, C♯/D♭	D♯/E♭, E
G (3rd) string	G	E, F, F♯/G♭	G♯/A♭, A
B (2nd) string	B	G♯/A♭, A, A♯/B♭	C, C♯/D♭
Both E strings (1st and 6th)	E	C♯/D♭, D, D♯/E♭	F, F♯/G♭

Again, once you've got the right note in the chromatic pitch indicator, then get the fine-tuning indicator right in the center. That's it!

Here's a general rule to follow regarding which way to turn your tuning keys.

HIGH E (1ST), B (2ND), AND G (3RD) STRINGS
If the pitch is **flat**, turn the tuner **clockwise**.

If the pitch is **sharp**, turn the tuner **counterclockwise**.

D (4TH), A (5TH), AND LOW E (6TH) STRINGS
If the pitch is **sharp**, turn the tuner **clockwise**.

If the pitch is **flat**, turn the tuner **counterclockwise**.

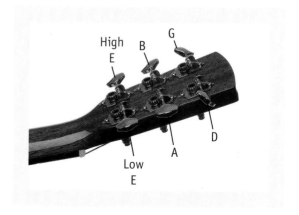

This method of tuning compares the string to be tuned with another string as a reference. It requires a bit more patience because you use your ear instead of an electronic tuner for guidance. You can use this technique once you have some more experience with the guitar.

Tune to Another Instrument

Here's a way to tune your guitar without an electronic tuner, or to another instrument. Assume that your bottom E string is in tune with another guitar or piano. You'll get the rest of the strings in tune based on this string's pitch.

① First, tune up the A (5th) string. Play the Low E (6th) string while putting a finger on the 5th fret. This note is an A, so you'll try to tune the open A string to this pitch.

② Now play the open A string.

If the open A string sounds higher than the Low E string, 5th fret, the A string is sharp. Lower the pitch by turning the A tuning peg clockwise until the two strings have the same pitch.

If the open A string sounds lower than the Low E string, 5th fret, the A string is flat. Tighten the A string by turning the A tuning key until the two strings have the same pitch.

③ Continue the process for the other strings. Hearing the subtle differences in pitch takes practice, but you can do it if you take your time and go slowly.

Tune the open D (4th) string to the A (5th) string, 5th fret.

④ Then tune the open G (3rd) string to the D (4th) string, 5th fret.

⑤ The only exception occurs when you tune the B (2nd) string. You tune the B string to the G (3rd) string, 4th fret.

⑥ Finally, tune the High E (1st) string to the B (2nd) string, 5th fret.

Steps 1–2. Tune open A to E string, 5th fret.

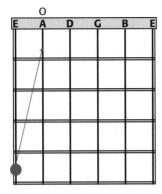

Step 3. Tune open D to A string, 5th fret.

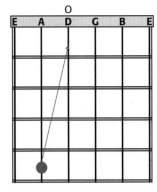

Step 4. Tune open G to D string, 5th fret.

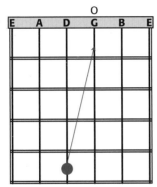

Step 5. Tune open B to G string, 4th fret.

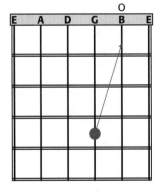

Step 6. Tune open High E to B string, 5th fret.

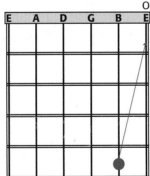

CHAPTER 4

Getting into Position

Before you start playing, take a moment to learn proper positioning. A few key reminders will help give your arms and hands more flexibility and reach.

Because guitarists and guitars come in all different shapes and sizes, you'll need to do a bit of experimenting to figure out what sitting position works best for you. Find a position that's easy on your hands, wrists, arms, and back.

Correct Sitting Position

When you're ready to start playing, you should be sitting in a comfortable position that allows you to access all parts of the guitar's neck without straining. Your back should be straight but relaxed. Your wrists should not be overly bent. Extreme angles in your wrists will impede the muscles in your hands.

If you are a steel-string player, let the lower curve of the guitar rest against the leg under your picking hand (the right leg if you are right-handed, or the left leg if you are left-handed).

Many guitarists are tempted to hunch over the guitar or tilt the guitar up toward them in order to see what their fingers are doing. Try to avoid these positions, which can put your neck, back, or wrists at awkward angles. Your fingers will eventually learn where chords and notes fall on the neck, and you'll get used to the viewing angle. The correct viewing angle is shown here.

Classical guitarists usually elevate the foot below the fretting hand (the left foot for a right-handed guitarist, or the right foot for a left-handed guitarist) on an adjustable footstool. By doing so, you can balance the guitar between your thighs, and your fretting hand can move freely across the neck. Your picking hand can also float freely above the strings, as is necessary for classical technique.

TIP

The fretting hand should not have to support or lift up the neck. Its only job is to press down on the strings. The guitar can be adequately cradled between your leg, chest, and upper arm.

Air Guitar Test

Before you pick up a guitar, try this air guitar test. Pretend you're playing the guitar without the instrument and look at the angles in your wrists.

Once you're satisfied that both hands feel relatively comfortable, have someone place the guitar in your hands. To rest the guitar in the position you've picked, you may have to alter your sitting position by shifting your legs or angling the guitar.

If you play an electric guitar, you may need the help of a strap to achieve the proper sitting position, because the relatively small size of an electric guitar's body may make it sit lower in your lap.

NOTE: Because many electric guitars have smaller bodies than their acoustic counterparts, you may have less surface area to balance the guitar properly when you sit. This makes using a strap when you play even more important.

Standing

The same principles of sitting apply to standing, except now you'll be using a guitar strap to help position the instrument. The strap puts the guitar in the easiest place for your arms and hands to move around.

Use a Guitar Strap

Many guitarists, especially those who also sing, prefer to stand rather than sit. You can use a guitar strap to help balance the guitar around your neck and back. One end of the strap goes around the end pin of the guitar.

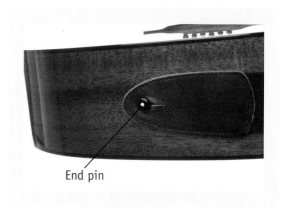

End pin

The other end of the strap can be tied around the neck by the tuning pegs (a) or hung around another pin where the neck meets the body (b).

NOTE: Tying the strap around the neck may impede your fretting hand, especially when you're playing open chords. Adding a neck pin is usually a quick and inexpensive modification for an acoustic guitar. Electric guitars come with two strap buttons; most acoustics have only one.

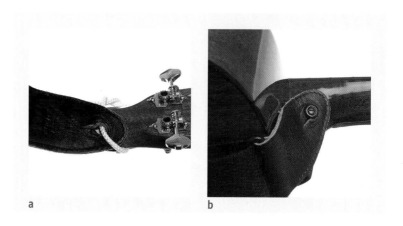

a

b

Hold the Guitar While Standing

As when sitting, make sure when you are standing that both of your hands can move comfortably across the guitar.

Depending how long your arms are, you may want to slightly angle the guitar neck so you can easily access all the parts of the fretboard.

Make sure the wrist of your fretting hand is not so low that it becomes crooked, which makes it hard to move your fingers. The photo gives you an example of a too low-slung neck.

You can use the same "air guitar" test as described for the sitting position to hoist the guitar to its proper placement.

Your fretting hand changes the pitch of the strings by placing pressure behind different frets. Here are some guidelines that will help you produce a clear tone with your fretting hand.

Fingers

Your fingertips should be placed directly behind any fret, without resting on top of the fret.

Your fingers should be gently curved unless you're playing a barre—in which a finger is laid across more than one string (see Chapter 11).

Correct   *Incorrect*

Use your fingertips, close to where the nail starts, but not your finger pads.

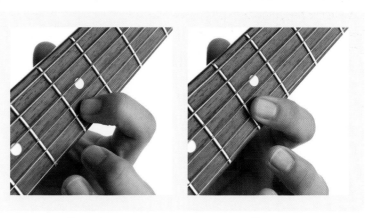

Correct   *Incorrect*

Thumb

Your thumb supports the fingers' pressure on the finger-board by pressing on the other side of the neck. For certain chords, the thumb may occasionally peek over the top of the neck. (You probably won't be able to do this on a nylon-string guitar, though, which has a wider neck than an electric or steel-string guitar.)

When playing barre chords (see Chapter 11), you'll want to keep your thumb behind the neck for extra support. When playing melodies, keeping your thumb in the back of the neck provides extra support and enables your fingers to stretch naturally along the length of the strings, as shown here.

TIP

When your thumb is behind the neck, make sure that your wrist doesn't bend severely as you change positions.

Avoid Fretting Position Problems

If you hear a muffled tone on a string, there are several things you can check. Here are some clues and solutions to fretting finger-position problems:

- Make sure you're putting enough pressure on the string. If you're not, you'll hear a muted, percussive clunk.

- Check that your finger is directly behind the fret. The farther the finger is from the fret, the more potential there is for the string in between to rattle. Photo a shows improper placement; photo b shows proper placement.

- Make sure that other fingers aren't touching the string, as in photo c. If you're playing with your fingertips, the other fingers will be arched over neighboring strings, as in photo d.

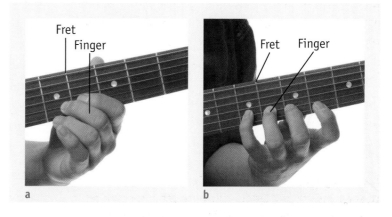

Fret
Finger
a

Fret   Finger
b

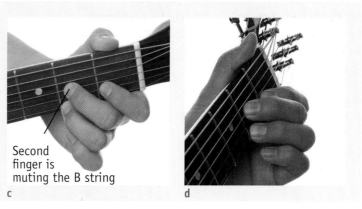

Second
finger is
muting the B string
c

d

Picking Hand Position

Your picking hand produces the string's tone. Whether you use your fingers (known as fingerpicking) or a pick, you'll want a stable reference point for your hand so that it can develop consistent muscle memory of where to go to find a specific string without excess motion.

Fingerpicking Position

For fingerpicking, you have several options on how to position your hand. Classical guitarists let their hand float freely above the soundhole, with their forearm braced against the upper bout of the guitar.

Other fingerpickers rest the heel of their palm on the bridge. Photo a shows how you should initially place the heel of your palm; photo b shows fingerpicking with the heel of the palm anchored.

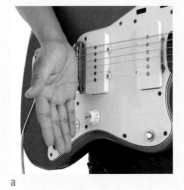

a

b

Some fingerpickers brace their ring finger or pinky on the face of the guitar, as shown here.

See Chapter 8 for more on fingerpicking.

Using a Pick

If you use a pick, the best place to position your hand is on the bridge. When you let the heel of your palm rest on the bridge, your hand can quickly pivot to any string. Using your pinky or ring finger can hinder this freedom of movement with a pick.

See Chapter 8 for more on how to use a pick.

CHAPTER 5

Your First Chords and Song

A chord is a set of three or more different notes that create a sense of harmony. After you learn how to use chord charts—maps of the fingerboard showing you which fingers to use and which strings to play—you'll be able to find all the chords you need. I'll start off by showing you D, A7, and G, the easiest chords to play in any key. At the end of the chapter, you'll put those three chords together in a simple song.

A chord chart is a map of the guitar's fingerboard. It shows you which fingers to use, where to place them, and which strings to play in order to play a particular chord. After you know the basics, you can use chord charts to teach yourself any chord.

VERTICAL LINES

From left to right, the vertical lines in a chord chart represent the Low E, A, D, G, B, and High E strings. The High E string, also called the 1st string, is the one closest to your feet when you play. The Low E, or 6th, string is closest to your face.

HORIZONTAL LINES

The top horizontal line represents the nut of the guitar. The horizontal line directly underneath it represents the 1st fret, and the lines below that represent the 2nd, 3rd, and 4th frets, respectively.

X'S AND 0'S

If you see an X above a string, you don't play that string. If you see an 0 above a string, it's an open string; that is, you play it, but you don't place a fretting-hand finger on it.

NUMBERED DOTS

A dot on the fretboard means that you put a finger there. The number in the dot tells you which fretting hand finger to use:

1 = index finger
2 = middle finger
3 = ring finger
4 = pinky

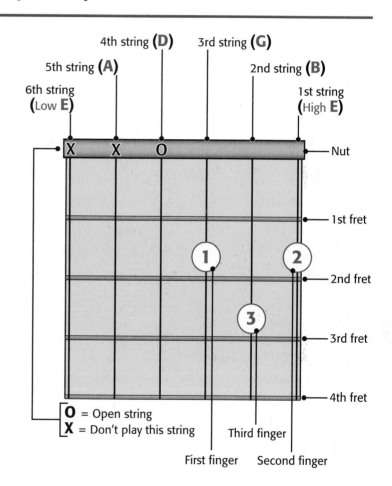

4th string **(D)**   3rd string **(G)**
5th string **(A)**   2nd string **(B)**
6th string   1st string
(Low **E**)   (High **E**)

Nut
1st fret
2nd fret
3rd fret
4th fret

0 = Open string
X = Don't play this string

First finger   Third finger   Second finger

D Chord

Here is the chart for the D chord. First, notice the X's above the Low E (6th) and A (5th) strings. The presence of these X's means that you don't strum or pick these strings at all. Next, notice the 0 above the D (4th) string. This 0 means you can play this string without having to put a fretting hand finger on it.

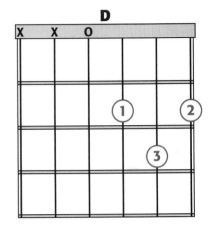

How to Finger the D Chord

There are three dots on the D chord chart, so you will place your first three fingers to correspond with those dots.

On the G (3rd) string, there is a dot on the 2nd fret. Because there is a 1 in that dot, you place your index finger on that spot, right behind the 2nd fret.

On the High E (1st) string, there is a dot on the 2nd fret. Because there is a 2 in that dot, you place your middle finger on that spot, right behind the 2nd fret.

Finally, on the B (2nd) string, there is a dot on the 3rd
fret. Because there is a 3 in that dot, you place your ring
finger on that spot, right behind the 3rd fret.

There's your D chord! Now just play the bottom four
strings. Remember, you're not playing the Low E (6th)
and A (5th) strings.

A7 Chord

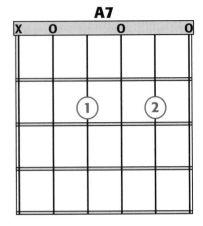

A7

Now try the same process with the A7 chord. Playing this chord requires only two fingers. You won't be playing the Low E (6th) string (notice the X on the far-left string), and you don't need to place fingers on the A (5th), G (3rd), and High E (1st) strings (notice the 0's on them).

How to Finger the A7 Chord

There is a dot on the 2nd fret of the D (4th) string. Because there is a 1 in that dot, you place your index finger on that spot, right behind the 2nd fret.

There is a dot on the 2nd fret of the B (2nd) string. Because there is a 2 in that dot, you place your middle finger on that spot, right behind the 2nd fret.

There's A7! Just strum the bottom five strings. Remember, you're not playing the Low E (6th) string.

Now let's play the G chord. Take a look at the chord chart at right and try it before looking at the photos below to see if you did it correctly.

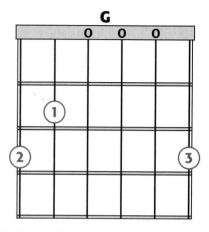

How to Finger the G Chord

The G chord uses all six strings; there are no X's in the chart. You play the D (4th), G (3rd), and B (2nd) strings open (no fingers) because of the O symbols at the top. Here's how you play this chord.

❶ Place your index finger on the 2nd fret of the A (5th) string.

❷ Place your middle finger on the 3rd fret of the Low E (6th) string.

❸ Finally, place your ring finger on the 3rd fret of the High E (1st) string.

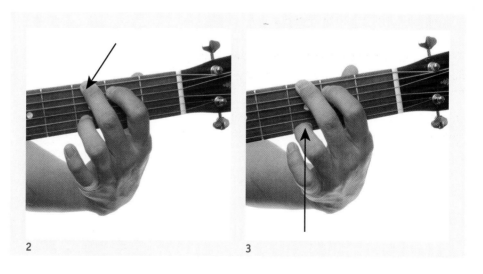

2

3

Put These Chords Together in a Song

Here's the moment you've been waiting for—your first song! Below you'll find what's known as a lead sheet, which maps out the chords of a song with the lyrics. "Sloop John B" is an old folk song that also has hit the pop charts. Chapter 10 goes into more detail about how to read a lead sheet, but for now, assume that every chord symbol means four beats. (See Chapter 9 for more on playing in time.) Take your time and play the song slowly at first.

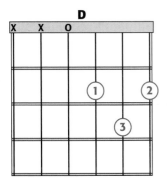
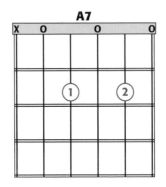
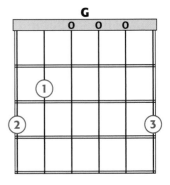

"Sloop John B"

INTRO

D	D
	We

VERSE 1

D	D		D	D	
come on the sloop John	B,	My	grandfather and	me, A-	
D	D		A7	A7	
round Nassau	town we did		roam.	Drinking all	
D	D		G	G	
night,	Got into a		fight.		Well I
D	A7		D	D	
feel so broke up,	I want to go		home.	So	

CHORUS

D	D		D	D	
hoist up the John B's	sail,		See how the mainsail	sets,	
D	D		A7	A7	
Call for the Captain a-	shore, Let me go		home,	let me go	

46

D	D	G	G
home,	I wanna go	home, yeah	yeah, Well I

D	A7	D	D
feel so broke up	I wanna go	home.	

VERSE 2

D	D	D	D
The first mate he got	drunk, And	broke in the Cap'n's	trunk, The

D	D	A7	A7
constable had to	come and take him a-	way.	Sheriff John

D	D	G	G
Stone,	Why don't you leave me a-	lone, yeah	yeah. Well I

D	A7	D	D
feel so broke up	I want to go	home.	So

CHORUS

D	D	D	D
hoist up the John B's	sail,	See how the mainsail	sets,

D	D	A7	A7
Call for the Captain a-	shore, Let me go	home,	let me go

D	D	G	G
home,	I wanna go	home, yeah	yeah, Well I

D	A7	D	D
feel so broke up	I wanna go	home.	The

VERSE 3

D	D	D	D
poor cook he caught the	fits And	threw away all my grits,	And

D	D	A7	A7
then he took and he	ate up all of my	corn.	Let me go

D	D	G	G
home,	Why don't they let me go	home?	This

D	A7	D	D
is the worst trip	I've ever been	on.	So

(Repeat chorus one more time)

CHAPTER 6

The Rest of the Open Chords

Open chords, like the D, A7, and G chords that you learned in Chapter 5, all have at least one open string that is played.

A

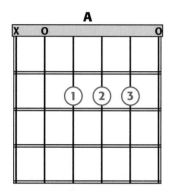

A

Play the bottom five strings (A–High E)

First finger on D (4th) string, 2nd fret

Second finger on G (3rd) string, 2nd fret

Third finger on B (2nd) string, 2nd fret

For the A7 chord, see Chapter 5.

 Am

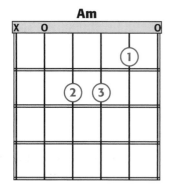

Play the bottom five strings (A–High E)

First finger on B (2nd) string, 1st fret

Second finger on D (4th) string, 2nd fret

Third finger on G (3rd) string, 2nd fret

6 🎤 **Am7**

Am7

Play the bottom five strings (A–High E)

First finger on B (2nd) string, 1st fret

Second finger on D (4th) string, 2nd fret

B7 Chord

B7

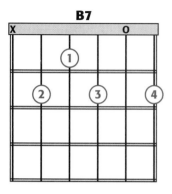

*Play the bottom five strings
(A–High E)*

*First finger on D (4th) string,
1st fret*

*Second finger on A (5th) string,
2nd fret*

*Third finger on G (3rd) string,
2nd fret*

*Fourth finger on High E (1st) string,
2nd fret*

C

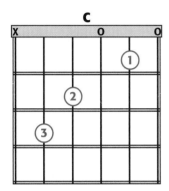

Play the bottom five strings (A–High E)

First finger on B (2nd) string, 1st fret

Second finger on D (4th) string, 2nd fret

Third finger on A (5th) string, 3rd fret

C7

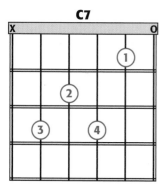

C7

Play the bottom five strings
(A–High E)

First finger on B (2nd) string,
1st fret

Second finger on D (4th) string,
2nd fret

Third finger on A (5th) string,
3rd fret

Fourth finger on G (3rd) string,
3rd fret

D7

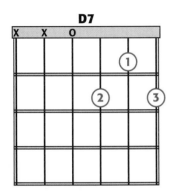

Play the bottom four strings (D–High E)

First finger on B (2nd) string, 1st fret

Second finger on G (3rd) string, 2nd fret

Third finger on High E (1st) string, 2nd fret

For the D chord, see Chapter 5.

Dm

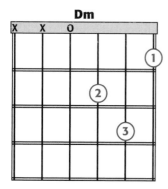

Play the bottom four strings (D–High E)

First finger on High E (1st) string, 1st fret

Second finger on G (3rd) string, 2nd fret

Third finger on B (2nd) string, 3rd fret

E

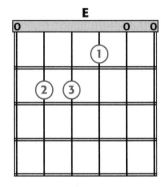

Play all six strings

First finger on G (3rd) string, 1st fret

Second finger on A (5th) string, 2nd fret

Third finger on D (4th) string, 2nd fret

E7

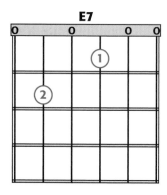

Play all six strings

First finger on G (3rd) string, 1st fret

Second finger on A (5th) string, 2nd fret

Em

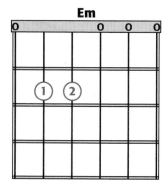

Play the bottom five strings (A–High E)

First finger on A (5th) string, 2nd fret

Second finger on D (4th) string, 2nd fret

Alternate Em

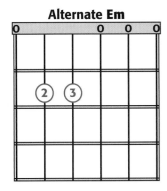

Alternate Em

Play all six strings

First finger on A (5th) string, 2nd fret

Second finger on D (4th) string, 2nd fret

 Em7

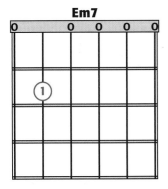

Em7

Play all six strings

First finger on A (5th) string, 2nd fret

G7 Chord

For the G chord, see Chapter 5.

11 🎤 G7

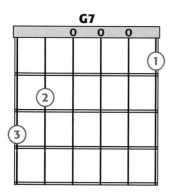

G7

Play all six strings

First finger on High E (1st) string, 1st fret

Second finger on A (5th) string, 2nd fret

Third finger on Low E (6th) string, 3rd fret

CHAPTER 7

Moving Between Chords

Now that you've learned the open chords (see Chapters 5 and 6), let's look at the best way to move between them. Whatever the chord combination, you'll want to find the most direct and efficient way of moving your fingers to and from each chord formation.

Economy of Motion

The more you move your fingers and hands, the more potential there is for error and delay. Do only the minimum lifting necessary to move your fingers in and out of different chord positions.

Relax Your Fingers

The less you have to move your fingers, the quicker you can transition between chords. When you lift your fingers, raise them just enough to clear the strings. You don't have to open your hand or pull your fingertip inches above the fingerboard. If you simply relax your hand, your fingers will lift up on the neck.

This photo shows too much lifting of the fingers when shifting chord positions.

Only a minimal amount of lifting is needed to change chord positions, as shown here.

Move to an Adjacent String

If you're moving to an adjacent string on the same fret, just shift your finger up or down after releasing the pressure. Photo a shows the first finger on the A (5th) string, 2nd fret. In photo b, that finger has shifted to the D (4th) string, 2nd fret.

a

b

If you're moving to an adjacent fret on the same string, slide your finger up or down the string after releasing the pressure.

Here you see the first finger on the G (3rd) string, 2nd fret.

In this photo, the first finger has slid to the G (3rd) string, 1st fret.

Chord Shifts with Common Fingering

S ome chord shifts are easy because certain fingers don't move between chords. The first three chords you learned—D, A7, and G—all allow the first finger to stay on the 2nd fret. We'll start by shifting from the G chord, shown here.

Shift from G to Em

In this example, the progression goes from G (shown above) to Em (E minor).

To play the Em chord, you don't need the second and third fingers to hold their positions in G, so relax those fingers, as shown here. Remember, you don't want to actively lift your fingers; doing so would just add one more task for your hand to do. Instead, relax your fingers, and they will naturally lift out of the way for you.

Now, without lifting your first finger, place your second finger back on the D (4th) string, 2nd fret, and you have your Em chord. Remember that you're pivoting on the first finger without lifting it.

Many beginner chord changes are easy because the fingers stay on a given fret. As mentioned on the previous page, the D, A7, and G chords all allow the first finger to stay on the 2nd fret. The D chord is shown here.

Shift from D to A7

In this example, the progression goes from D (shown above) to A7.

You don't need your third finger to play the A7, so relax that finger and let it rise up and out of the way, as shown here. Remember, don't actively lift it; doing so would just add one more task for your hand to do.

Move the remaining two fingers up one string each. Both fingers stay on the same fret. The first finger moves from the G (3rd) string to the D (4th) string, and the second finger moves from the High E (1st) string to the B (2nd) string. Try moving the two fingers as a unit. Just shift them upward to their new strings. You don't have to lift them more than a few millimeters (a).

Now press down, and you're at the A7 chord (b)!

a

b

Chord Shifts on the Same String

Many beginner chord changes are easy because one finger stays on a given string in both chords. In these cases, you don't need to lift that finger.

Shift from D to E7

Moving from D to E7 is an example of a chord change in which a finger remains on a string. Here's the D chord fingering (a).

From the D chord, relax your second and third fingers and allow them to lift slightly (b).

a

b

The first finger slides from the 2nd fret to the 1st fret of the G (3rd) string (c). Remember, you don't have to lift this finger at all. Just let it slide on the surface of the string back one fret toward the nut.

Now add the second finger to the A (5th) string, 2nd fret (d). This is the shape for E7. On this chord, you strum all six strings.

c

d

Move from Chord to Chord without a Common String

When you're moving from chord to chord, especially when the two chords don't have a common fret or string, you'll find it helpful to try two ways of moving your fingers. Either of these methods may be easier for your fingers for any given chord combination. Whatever method works for you is fine; work with your muscle tendencies instead of fighting them.

Move Your First Finger First

Many people are most adept with their first finger because of its predominance in everyday use. Concentrate on moving your first finger to its appropriate place in the destination chord, and then place your other fingers.

For example, if you're playing A7 (a) to E7 (b), you would move your first finger from the D (4th) string, 2nd fret, to the G (3rd) string, 1st fret. Then move your other finger, from the B (2nd) string, 2nd fret, to the A (5th) string, 2nd fret.

a

b

Move Your Farthest Finger First

Your "farthest" finger is the finger that wraps around the guitar the most and is closest to your thumb. Because this finger has to do the most traveling across the neck, for many people it makes sense to move it before the others. Concentrate on moving your farthest finger to its appropriate place in the destination chord, and then place the other fingers.

For example, if you're playing A7 to E7, the second finger of E7 is the farthest across the neck, so

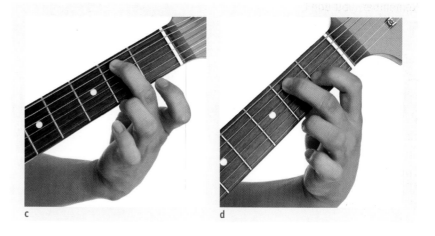

c   d

you would move that finger first. Move it from the B (2nd) string, 2nd fret, to the A (5th) string, 2nd fret (c). Then move your first finger from the D (4th) string, 2nd fret, to the G (3rd) string, 1st fret (d).

A Practice Strategy

If you're having trouble moving between two particular chords, try adding fingers to the destination chord. For example, if you're having trouble moving between G and A, try alternating between the G chord (a) and just the first finger of the A chord (b). Strum all the same strings you would normally play for now.

Once your fingers are used to that transition (c), go ahead and add the next finger (d).

Once you can transition both of those fingers in the A chord smoothly (e), add the last finger to the A chord (f).

Using this method helps the individual fingers learn their muscle memory gradually.

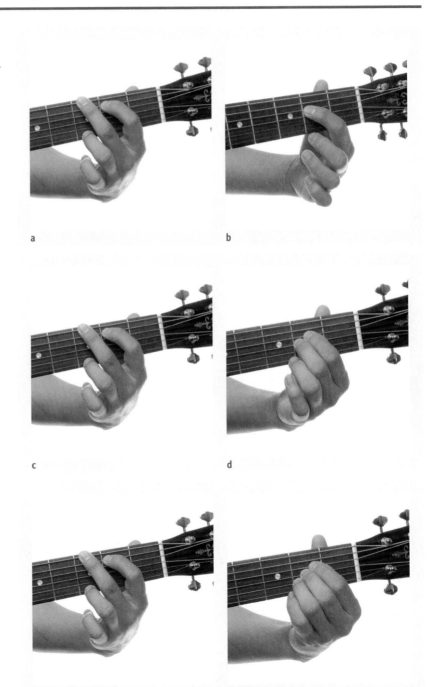

a

b

c

d

e

f

CHAPTER 8

Strumming and Picking

The hand that's not on the fretboard is in charge of the guitar's rhythm. Whether you use your fingers or a pick, this hand has the job of making your guitar groove and move in time.

Start with Your Thumb

Because you're still getting used to forming chords, we'll start with the most basic strumming-hand technique: using the pad of your thumb to strum chords. Using the outer, or higher, edge of your thumb pad as you begin to play chords produces a warm sound.

G Chord Strum

Start with the G chord, which uses all six strings.

1. Relax your arm and wrist. A tense arm or wrist results in a stiff sound.

2. Allow your thumb to hover above the Low E (6th) string.

3. Let your thumb drop from the Low E (6th) string all the way to the High E (1st) string, giving all six strings the same amount of vibration.

   At the end of the strum, your thumb should be clear of the High E (1st) string, but not too far away from it, as shown here.

Strumming Other Chords

A CHORD STRUM 1

What if the chord you're playing doesn't use all six strings? Let's try an A chord, which uses the bottom five strings. Relax your arm and wrist again and allow your thumb to rest on the A (5th) string.

A CHORD STRUM 2

Let the thumb drop from the A (5th) string all the way to the High E (1st) string, giving all five strings the same amount of vibration. At the end of the strum, your thumb should be clear of the High E (1st) string, but not too far away from it.

D CHORD STRUM 1

For a D chord, which uses the bottom four strings, relax your arm and wrist again and allow your thumb to rest on the D (4th) string.

D CHORD STRUM 2

Let the thumb drop from the D (4th) string all the way to the High E (1st) string, giving all four strings the same amount of vibration.

Play with a Pick

Playing with a pick helps you focus your sound and enables you to play faster rhythms. If you're a beginner, using a pick may feel strange at first, but you'll soon learn to strum and pick individual notes.

Most picks today are made of plastic or nylon and come in a variety of sizes and thicknesses. Thinner picks may be easier for beginners to use because of their lightness and flexibility. Thicker picks sound fuller against the strings and can execute faster passages of notes.

Pick Strum

① Hold the pick between the side of your first finger and the pad of your thumb. Grip about two-thirds of the pick surface, allowing the tip of the pick to strike the strings.

② Try not to tense your wrist and arm as you hold the pick. You won't be able to play dynamically and sensitively if your arm can't absorb the vibration from the strings. When you strum down (a) and up (b), your wrist should move more than your arm.

a

b

Anchor and Mute

ANCHOR

When you play individual strings for arpeggios (broken chords) or melodies, you may want to anchor your hand on the bridge. Doing so will give you a consistent place to pick from, and your hand will get used to picking from one place and develop muscle memory.

Down stroke

Up stroke

MUTE

When you want a chunkier or drumlike sound, you can use this position for a technique called *muting*. By slightly pressing down with the fleshy part of your palm on the string where it meets the bridge, you can create a more percussive, yet muted sound.

Fingerpicking

Fingerpicking allows the guitar's interlocking sonic qualities to come out. By learning basic patterns, you can synchronize your thumb and finger motions to play simple arrangements of notes.

Fingerpicking Technique (Arpeggio)

Fingerpicking involves using the thumb and fingertips together. You've already started to use your thumb, so let's refine the technique. For fingerpicking, you use the junction of where your nail meets the skin to hit the string. The nail helps project the tone, while the skin gives the tone warmth.

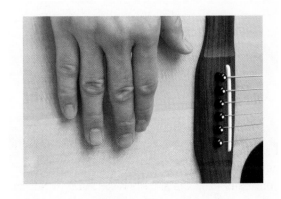

Try a G chord. Your thumb plays the Low E (6th) string, while your first and second fingers play the G (3rd) and B (2nd) strings, respectively.

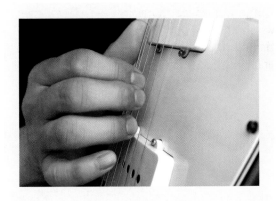

First, let your thumb fall as it plucks the Low E (6th) string. You don't have to pull up on the string. Allow gravity to pull the thumb down.

Use your first finger to play the G (3rd) string. The finger should simply close in to the palm, without lifting your hand from the surface of the guitar. Notice that the top of the hand doesn't rise.

Now use your second finger to play the B (2nd) string. Again, the finger should simply close in to the palm. You've just played an *arpeggio*—a broken chord figure in which notes are played individually (one string at a time) instead of simultaneously. Repeat this pattern several times to create a cyclical, rhythmic effect.

TIP

Tone production is an important part of fingerpicking technique. Think of brushing as opposed to plucking when your fingers touch the strings. Try not to lift your hand every time you play a note. Instead, use the separate motions of the fingers and thumb, not the hand and forearm, to do the work. If you're getting too much of a plucking sound, use less nail and more skin when you contact the string.

Fingerpicking *(continued)*

Fingerpicking in Tablature

The pattern you learned earlier in this chapter isn't the only pattern you can use for fingerpicking. You can call that first pattern T 1 2, since your order of picking is thumb, first finger, second finger. After you learn how to read tablature (see Chapter 10), you can combine that skill with fingerpicking to play new patterns.

Usually, you want to play the *root* of a chord—the note with the same name as the chord—with your thumb. For example, the root of the Em chord is E, and the root of the D (major) chord is D. The chart at right shows you where the roots of different chords are found.

Chord	Thumb Plays Root on This String
E, E7, Em	Low E (6th)
G, G7	Low E (6th)
A, A7, Am	A (5th)
B7	A (5th)
C, C7	A (5th)
D, D7	D (4th)

Fingerpicking Patterns: "House of the Rising Sun"

You can apply a variety of fingerpicking patterns to "House of the Rising Sun," a popular song from the 1960s. The fingerpicking patterns appear on the pages following the song. Here are the chords you'll need:

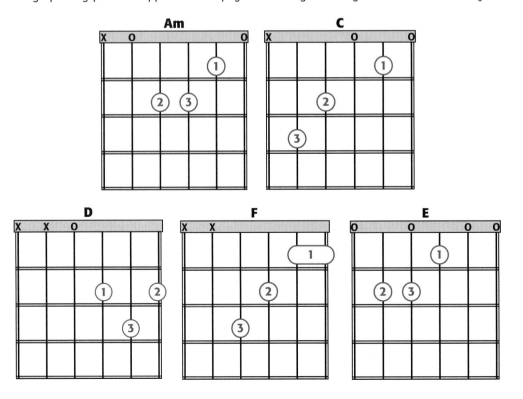

Am	Am
	There

VERSE 1

Am	C	D	F
is a	house in	New Orleans	They

Am	C	E	E
call the	Rising	Sun,	and it's

Am	C	D	F
been the	ruin of	many a poor	boy, and

Am	E	Am	E
God, I	know I'm	one.	My

VERSE 2

Am	C	D	F
mother	was a	tailor	She

Am	C	E	E
sewed my	new blue-	jeans.	My

Am	C	D	F
father	was a	gamblin'	man

Am	E	Am	E
Down in	New Or-	leans.	Now the

VERSE 3

Am	C	D	F
only	thing a	gambler needs	is a

Am	C	E	E
suitcase	and a	trunk.	And the

Am	C	D	F
only	time he's	satisfied.	Is

Am	E	Am	E
when he's	on a	drunk.	Oh

VERSE 4

Am	C	D	F
mother	tell your	children	not to

Am	C	E	E
do what	I have	done.	

Am	C	D	F	
Spend your	lives in	sin and miser-	y,	in the

Am	E	Am	E
House of the	Rising	Sun.	There

VERSE 1

Am	C	D	F
is a	house in	New Orleans	They

Am	C	E	E
call the	Rising	Sun,	and it's

Am	C	D	F
been the	ruin of	many a poor	boy, and

Am	E	Am
God, I	know I'm	one.

⑬ 🎤 T 1 2 FINGERPICKING PATTERN

Here is a thumb (T or 0), first (1), and second (2) fingerpicking pattern for "House of the Rising Sun." The thumb plays either the D (4th), A (5th), or Low E (6th) string; the first finger plays the G (3rd) string; and the second finger plays the B (2nd) string. Each row of photos shows you the left-hand chord fingering, and then the thumb stroke, first finger stroke, and second finger stroke on the picking hand.

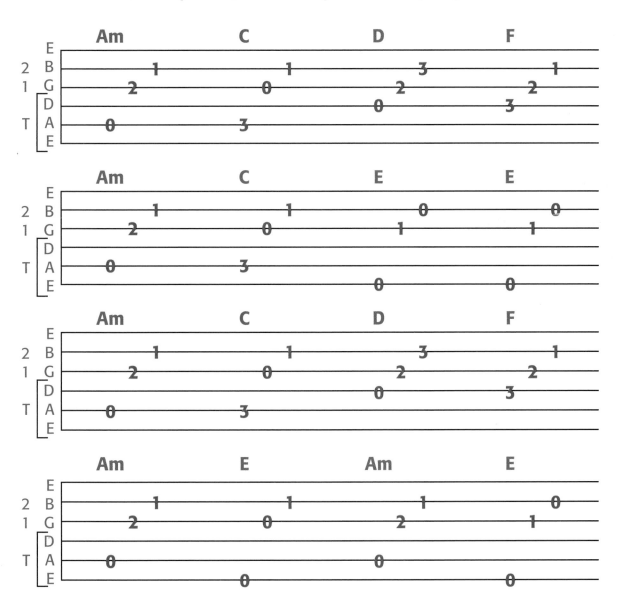

CHORD	THUMB	1ST FINGER	2ND FINGER

A MINOR

  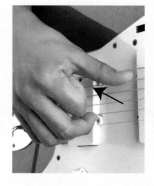 

C

  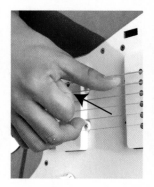 

D

  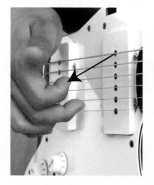 

CHORD	THUMB	1ST FINGER	2ND FINGER

E

F

Fingerpicking *(continued)*

14 ⏺ T 1 2 3 FINGERPICKING PATTERN

Here is a thumb (T or 0), first (1), second (2), and third (3) fingerpicking pattern. The pattern is similar to the one you just did, but now the third finger plays the High E (1st) string.

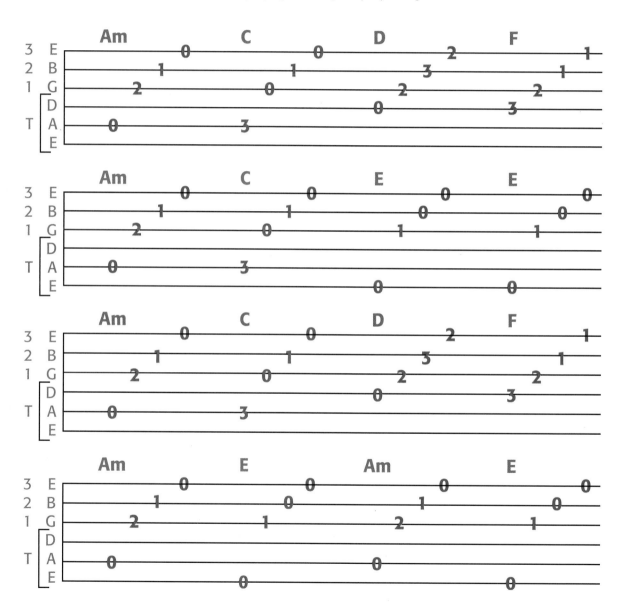

CHAPTER 9

Rhythm Guitar

Now that you know the open chords and know how to strum those chords, let's put the two together. Rhythm guitar is how you play chords in various rhythms to accompany a song's melody.

The Basics of Tempo

The rate at which a song is played is called the tempo. Keeping a steady tempo—not speeding up or slowing down within a given tune—is one of the challenges of playing rhythm guitar, especially for a beginner. As a song progresses, most guitarists find that they want to speed up (though some tend to slow down). This is a natural impulse when performing a repetitive function like strumming. Also, when guitarists reach the chorus of a song, they often react to the song's natural surge and play faster. This section outlines some techniques that make playing in time easier.

Keeping Time with Your Foot

The best way to combat the natural tendency to speed up is to tap your foot in time during a song. Pretend that you're walking down the street. You usually don't vary your speed when you walk unless you make a conscious decision to do so. Since you've been walking longer than you've been playing guitar, your feet have very good muscle memory of keeping time.

Some people feel awkward tapping their toes. Here are some alternate ways of keeping time:

- Tap your toe inside of your shoe.
- Tap your heel.
- Alternately tap your left and right feet, as if you were walking down the street.
- Rock from side to side in your chair, as if you were dancing.

> **TIP**
>
> Pretend that you've got a piece of string tied between your tapping foot and your strumming hand. You can use this imaginary piece of string to synchronize the time in your foot to the time in your strumming hand.

Most of today's popular music uses the 4/4 time signature. This section explains how and where to divide up and emphasize your strumming to propel your guitar playing in 4/4 time.

Breaking Down 4/4 Time

The basic unit of rhythmic measurement is called a *bar*. In the 4/4 time signature, the rhythm is comprised of four beats per bar:

Beats:	1	2	3	4	|1	2	3	4 etc.
	First bar				Second bar			

The first beat of each bar usually gets the most rhythmic emphasis. (One notable exception is reggae, where the guitar and bass often do not play on the first beat.) The third beat is usually the second-most emphasized note.

You synchronize the four beats of each bar with your foot taps. The halfway points between these beats are called "ands" and are represented by + symbols in the graphic below. Notice that the ands happen between the down taps of the foot, when the foot comes back up

Beats:	1	+	2	+	3	+	4	+
Foot:	Down	Up	Down	Up	Down	Up	Down	Up

When your foot goes down, you strum down.

When your foot lifts up, you strum up.

4/4 Strumming Patterns

Now let's take the information about 4/4 time and start strumming. Use your foot tapping as a guide so you don't lose your sense of tempo.

DOWN STRUMS ONLY

Start by playing a simple strum on the first beat of each bar. Finger the G chord (see Chapter 5) and strum when you see the V symbol. The V symbol indicates that you should play a down stroke, where the pick goes from the Low E (6th) string all the way to the High E (1st) string. Remember to keep time by tapping your foot and down strum when the first of the four foot taps occurs. Repeat this pattern several times:

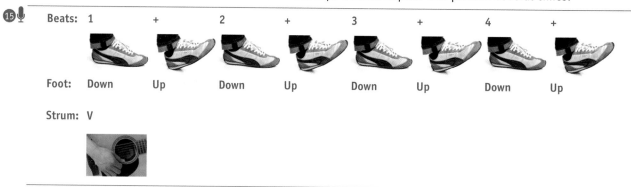

Beats:	1	+	2	+	3	+	4	+
Foot:	Down	Up	Down	Up	Down	Up	Down	Up
Strum:	V							

Once you feel you can play this strum in time, you can start subdividing the bar. The halfway point of the bar is the third beat. Add a down strum on the third beat, but let the first beat be the more prominent one by giving that strum a bit more emphasis. Again, you're strumming only on the first and third foot taps. Repeat this pattern several times:

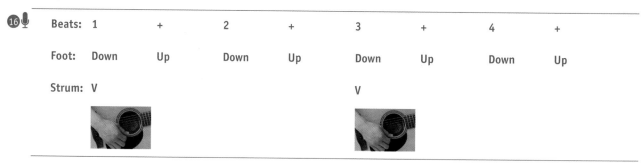

Beats:	1	+	2	+	3	+	4	+
Foot:	Down	Up	Down	Up	Down	Up	Down	Up
Strum:	V				V			

Keep going to get an even fuller rhythm pattern sound. Again, subdivide the bar. In other words, add a down strum on the second and fourth beats, keeping the strum on the first beat the most prominent. Now, every time your foot comes down, you're doing a down strum at the same time:

17

Beats:	1	+	2	+	3	+	4	+
Foot:	Down	Up	Down	Up	Down	Up	Down	Up
Strum:	V		V		V		V	

DOWN STRUMS AND UP STRUMS

Now try adding up strums, indicated by the ^ symbols. Every time your foot comes down, you do a down strum at the same time, and every time your foot comes up, you do an up strum. When you play this set of alternating down strums and up strums, you are playing an eight-note pattern:

18

Beats:	1	+	2	+	3	+	4	+
Foot:	Down	Up	Down	Up	Down	Up	Down	Up
Strum:	V	^	V	^	V	^	V	^

To make this pattern sound more urgent, especially for rock rhythms, you can make all the strums down strums: Do a down strum when your foot goes down, and a down strum when it comes up. This is a great rhythm in which to make a more percussive sound by slightly muting the strings where they meet the bridge (see the section "Anchor and Mute" in Chapter 8):

19

Beats:	1	+	2	+	3	+	4	+
Foot:	Down	Up	Down	Up	Down	Up	Down	Up
Strum:	V	V	V	V	V	V	V	V

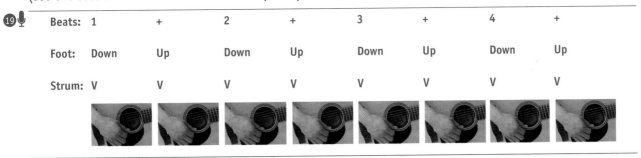

You can make other patterns that don't sound as busy or cluttered by removing some of the up strokes:

20 🎤

Beats:	1	+	2	+	3	+	4	+
Foot:	Down	Up	Down	Up	Down	Up	Down	Up
Strum:	V		V	^	V	^	V	^

21 🎤

Beats:	1	+	2	+	3	+	4	+
Foot:	Down	Up	Down	Up	Down	Up	Down	Up
Strum:	V	^	V		V	^	V	^

SYNCOPATED PATTERNS

Other patterns are less rhythmically obvious, or sound *syncopated*. Syncopation occurs when the ear is drawn to a beat that is normally not emphasized. In other words, you syncopate the rhythm by drawing attention to certain up beats. Even common pop and rock music contains syncopation, although it may be very subtle.

Syncopation removes some of the prominent down beats, which is what's happening in the pattern below. This example eliminates the down strum on beat 3.

22 🎤

Beats:	1	+	2	+	3	+	4	+
Foot:	Down	Up	Down	Up	Down	Up	Down	Up
Strum:	V	^	V	^		^	V	^

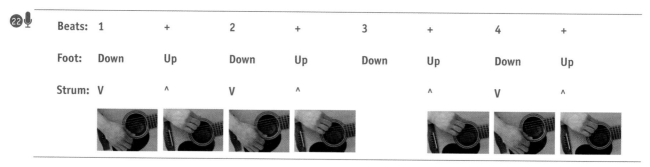

This example eliminates the down strum on beat 4.

23

Beats:	1	+	2	+	3	+	4	+
Foot:	Down	Up	Down	Up	Down	Up	Down	Up
Strum:	V	^	V	^	V	^		^

Here's another syncopated rhythm pattern to practice, eliminating the down strum on the 2nd and 4th beats.

24

Beats:	1	+	2	+	3	+	4	+
Foot:	Down	Up	Down	Up	Down	Up	Down	Up
Strum:	V	^		^	V	^		^

TIP

Keeping a proper tempo is one of the hardest things for many musicians to master. Playing with a *metronome*, a device that produces a steady beat that you can play against, is a great way to develop the ability to play in time.

3/4 Time

The second most common time signature is 3/4. It is commonly known as waltz time. As the name suggests, there are only three beats per bar. As in 4/4 time, the first beat gets the most emphasis (think "ONE-two-three ONE-two-three . . ."). Pop songs in 3/4 time include the Righteous Brothers' "Unchained Melody," Billy Joel's "Piano Man," and "Breaking the Girl" by the Red Hot Chili Peppers.

3/4 Strumming Patterns

This example has a down strum (as indicated by the V symbol) on the first, second, and third beats.

Beats:	1	+	2	+	3	+
Foot:	Down	Up	Down	Up	Down	Up
Strum:	V		V		V	

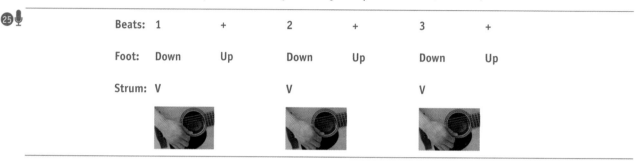

This example adds up strums (indicated by the ^ symbols) on the "ands" of the second and third beats.

Beats:	1	+	2	+	3	+
Foot:	Down	Up	Down	Up	Down	Up
Strum:	V		V	^	V	^

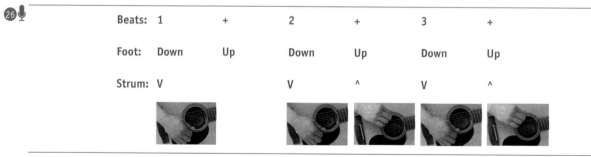

This example adds up strums after each of the three beats.

Beats:	1	+	2	+	3	+
Foot:	Down	Up	Down	Up	Down	Up
Strum:	V	^	V	^	V	^

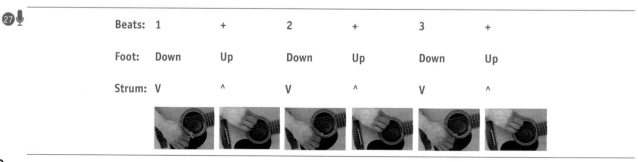

CHAPTER 10

Reading Chord Symbols, Tablature, and Lead Sheets

You've learned how to play some chords already. In this chapter, you'll learn how to read chords and their symbols. You'll also learn how to read tablature, a graphic representation of how melodies are played on the fingerboard.

Five Common Types of Guitar Chords

Chords have a specific language of symbols used to represent different sounds. Here's how to decipher the symbols for major, minor, dominant seventh, major seventh, and minor seventh chords.

Major Chords

Major chords are known for their generally bright, happy sound. The 12 major chords are:

C
C♯ or D♭ (same chord with two potential names)
D
D♯ or E♭ (same chord with two potential names)
E
F
F♯ or G♭ (same chord with two potential names)
G
G♯ or A♭ (same chord with two potential names)
A
A♯ or B♭ (same chord with two potential names)
B

Seven notes are referred to as *natural notes*. They have names just like the first seven letters of the alphabet: A, B, C, D, E, F, and G.

If you want to describe that a note is higher than a natural note, you attach the sharp sign: ♯. For example, the next note higher than F is F♯ (F sharp).

If you want to describe that a note is lower than a natural note, you attach the flat sign: ♭. For example, the next note lower than E is E♭ (E flat).

Notice that there is a major chord based on every one of the notes of the chromatic scale. There are 12 notes in the chromatic scale, from lowest to highest:

C, C♯ or D♭*, D, D♯ or E♭*, E, F, F♯ or G♭*, G, G♯ or A♭*, A, A♯ or B♭*, B

*The two alternate names of this note are referred to *enharmonic notes*. Generally, you won't use both sharp and flat note names in a single scale; you'll use one or the other.

Notice that there are no sharps or flats between E and F or between B and C.

Also notice that the chord symbol doesn't need the word *major* or *maj* after it; that is, the major chord based on C is notated as "C" instead of "C major" or "C maj."

The C, D, E, G, and A chords are all considered "open" major chords because at least one open string (a string with no fretting fingers on it) is being played. All the other major chords must be played as *barre chords,* in which your first finger extends over more than one string. (Barre chords are discussed in Chapter 11.)

D chord

Minor Chords

Minor chords are known for their generally dark, sad sound. The 12 minor chords are:

Cm

C♯m or D♭m (same chord with two potential names)

Dm

D♯m or E♭m (same chord with two potential names)

Em

Fm

F♯m or G♭m (same chord with two potential names)

Gm

G♯m or A♭m (same chord with two potential names)

Am

A♯m or B♭m (same chord with two potential names)

Bm

Notice that the chord symbol includes a lowercase *m* to signify that it's a minor chord. The chord doesn't need the word *minor* or *min* after it; the symbol for the minor chord based on A is notated as "Am," not "A minor" or "A min."

The Am, Dm, and Em chords are all considered "open" minor chords; all the other minor chords must be played as barre chords (see Chapter 11).

Am chord

Dominant and Major Seventh Chords

A seventh chord is a major chord with an extra note added. Seventh chords are used for several different purposes, such as to help one chord resolve to another.

Sometimes seventh chords are used because they have a funky, unstable sound. Suppose you have a progression that goes from A to D to E, then back to A—a relatively regular progression. Now make all the chords into seventh chords: A7 to D7 to E7, then back to A7. Your progression sounds much more bluesy with your chord modifications.

DOMINANT SEVENTH CHORDS

A *dominant seventh chord* has the same "happy" sound as a major chord but sounds less resolved, as if the chord were asking a question. Dominant seventh chords are common in blues, jazz, and R&B chord progressions. Notice that the chord symbol includes a 7 to signify that it's a seventh chord. The 12 dominant seventh chords are:

C7

C♯7 or D♭7 (same chord with two potential names)

D7

D♯7 or E♭7 (same chord with two potential names)

E7

F7

F♯7 or G♭7 (same chord with two potential names)

G7

G♯7 or A♭7 (same chord with two potential names)

A7

A♯7 or B♭7 (same chord with two potential names)

B7

The C7, D7, E7, G7, A7, and B7 chords can be played as open chords. All the other dominant seventh chords must be played as barre chords (see Chapter 11).

A7 chord

MAJOR SEVENTH CHORDS

A *major seventh chord* sounds more wistful and sentimental than a major chord, with a slightly sad feel. You can start and end a song on a major seventh chord, but it will sound melancholy and jazzy. The 12 major seventh chords are:

Cmaj7

C♯maj7 or D♭maj7 (same chord with two potential names)

Dmaj7

D♯maj7 or E♭maj7 (same chord with two potential names)

Emaj7

Fmaj7

F♯maj7 or G♭maj7 (same chord with two potential names)

Gmaj7

G♯maj7 or A♭maj7 (same chord with two potential names)

Amaj7

A♯maj7 or B♭maj7 (same chord with two potential names)

Bmaj7

Cmaj7, Dmaj7, Emaj7, Fmaj7, and Amaj7 can be played as chords; all the other major seventh chords must be played as barre chords (see Chapter 11).

Cmaj7 chord

Minor Seventh Chords

Minor seventh chords are minor chords with an extra note added. They are usually not as dark or intense as regular minor chords. They're often used in jazz, ballads, and more traditional popular music. The 12 minor seventh chords are:

Cm7

C#m7 or D♭m7 (same chord with two potential names)

Dm7

D#m7 or E♭m7 (same chord with two potential names)

Em7

Fm7

F#m7 or G♭m7 (same chord with two potential names)

Gm7

G#m7 or A♭m7 (same chord with two potential names)

Am7

A#m7 or B♭m7 (same chord with two potential names)

Bm7

Notice that the chord symbol includes the m7 to signify that it's a minor seventh chord. The Am7, Dm7, and Em7 chords are all considered "open" minor seventh chords; all the other minor seventh chords must be played as barre chords (see Chapter 11).

Am7 chord

Tablature is a notation system that shows the guitar's frets and strings and tells you where to place your fingers. Before you go very far in learning how to fingerpick or play melodies, it is useful to understand tablature.

What Tablature Shows You

Tablature tells you where on the fingerboard to play notes. It doesn't tell you how long to play each note or which finger to use.

Tablature uses six parallel lines. The top line represents the High E (1st) string, and the lower lines represent the B (2nd), G (3rd), D (4th), A (5th), and Low E (6th) strings. Events in tablature are read from left to right.

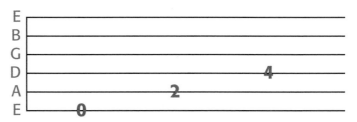

In this example, the first thing that you see is a 0 on the Low E (6th) string. The 0 indicates that you play the open string—that is, a string with no frets depressed.

To the right of that is a 2 on the A (5th) string. This 2 means that you place a finger on the 2nd fret of the A string and then play the A string. You can use any finger, but for now use your first finger.

Finally, you see a 4 on the D (4th) string. This 4 means that you put a finger on the 4th fret of the D string and then play the D string. Use your third finger to play that fret since it's an easy reach from the first finger on the A string.

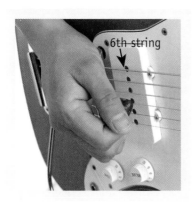

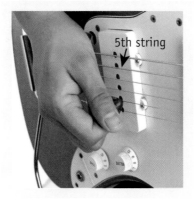

Chords in Tablature

29 If you see numbers lined up on top of one another, as below, the notes should be played simultaneously in a single strum. These fingerings form a D chord.

```
E ─────────────────2──────────────
B ─────────────────3──────────────
G ─────────────────2──────────────
D ─────────────────0──────────────
A ────────────────────────────────
E ────────────────────────────────
```

30 The tablature below shows that this chord is played as an arpeggio (see Chapter 12), because you play one note after another rather than play the notes simultaneously.

```
E ─────────────────────────2──────
B ───────────────────3─────────────
G ─────────────2───────────────────
D ───────0──────────────────────────
A ────────────────────────────────
E ────────────────────────────────
```

4th string

3rd string

2nd string

1st string

Play a Song from a Lead Sheet

A lead sheet allows you to play a song by mapping out the chords with the lyrics. This chapter illustrates how to read these charts.

Here's a lead sheet for "Sloop John B," a folk song that hit the pop charts when released by the Beach Boys on *Pet Sounds*. Following this lead sheet is an explanation of how to read it.

31 🎤 **INTRO**

D	D		
	We		

VERSE 1

D	D	D	D
come on the sloop John	B,	My grandfather and	me, A-
D	**D**	**A7**	**A7**
round Nassau	town we did	roam.	Drinking all
D	**D**	**G**	**G**
night,	Got into a	fight.	Well I
D	**A7**	**D**	**D**
feel so broke up,	I want to go	home.	So

CHORUS

D	D	D	D
hoist up the John B's	sail,	See how the mainsail	sets,
D	**D**	**A7**	**A7**
Call for the Captain a-	shore, Let me go	home,	let me go
D	**D**	**G**	**G**
home,	I wanna go	home, yeah	yeah, Well I
D	**A7**	**D**	**D**
feel so broke up	I wanna go	home.	

VERSE 2

D	D	D	D
The first mate he got	drunk, And	broke in the Cap'n's	trunk, The
D	**D**	**A7**	**A7**
constable had to	come and take him a-	way.	Sheriff John
D	**D**	**G**	**G**
Stone,	Why don't you leave me a-	lone, yeah	yeah. Well I
D	**A7**	**D**	**D**
feel so broke up	I want to go	home.	So

CHORUS

D	D	D	D
hoist up the John B's	sail,	See how the mainsail	sets,

D	D	A7	A7
Call for the Captain a-	shore, Let me go	home,	let me go

D	D	G	G
home,	I wanna go	home, yeah	yeah, Well I

D	A7	D	D
feel so broke up	I wanna go	home.	The

VERSE 3

D	D	D	D
poor cook he caught the	fits And	threw away all my	grits, And

D	D	A7	A7
then he took and he	ate up all of my	corn.	Let me go

D	D	G	G
home,	Why don't they let me go	home?	This

D	A7	D	D
is the worst trip	I've ever been	on.	So

CHORUS

D	D	D	D
hoist up the John B's	sail,	See how the mainsail	sets,

D	D	A7	A7
Call for the Captain a-	shore, Let me go	home,	let me go

D	D	G	G
home,	I wanna go	home, yeah	yeah, Well I

D	A7	D	D
feel so broke up	I wanna go	home.	

As with many pop songs, this tune is 4/4. (See Chapter 9 for an introduction to tempo and 4/4 time.) Remember, this means that bars are generally divided into groups of four, and the rhythmic emphasis is on the first beat.

Let's look at the song's introduction, which has two bars of D, and the first four bars of the verse, also on D.

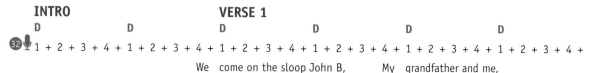

INTRO   **VERSE 1**

D   D   D   D   D   D

1 + 2 + 3 + 4 + 1 + 2 + 3 + 4 + 1 + 2 + 3 + 4 + 1 + 2 + 3 + 4 + 1 + 2 + 3 + 4 + 1 + 2 + 3 + 4 +

We   come on the sloop John B,   My   grandfather and me,

Don't worry too much about trying to synchronize your singing and playing when you first start out. You can use the word or syllable that lands on the first beat as a way to make sure your words are in time with the guitar. Remember, however, that the sung melody doesn't always start on the first beat. In this case, the word *We* actually starts before the first beat of the verse.

Start by playing a down stroke on the first beat of each bar.

INTRO   **VERSE 1**

D   D   D   D   D   D

1 + 2 + 3 + 4 + 1 + 2 + 3 + 4 + 1 + 2 + 3 + 4 + 1 + 2 + 3 + 4 + 1 + 2 + 3 + 4 + 1 + 2 + 3 + 4 +

V   V   V   V   V   V

We   come on the sloop John B,   My   grandfather and me,

Now add the third beat, but make the first beat more prominent by strumming slightly harder or by emphasizing the bass strings of the D chords (the D and G strings).

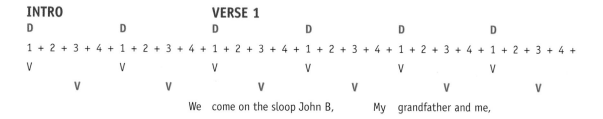

INTRO   **VERSE 1**

D   D   D   D   D   D

1 + 2 + 3 + 4 + 1 + 2 + 3 + 4 + 1 + 2 + 3 + 4 + 1 + 2 + 3 + 4 + 1 + 2 + 3 + 4 + 1 + 2 + 3 + 4 +

V   V   V   V   V   V

      V   V   V   V   V   V

We   come on the sloop John B,   My   grandfather and me,

Play a Song from a Lead Sheet *(continued)*

Now add the second and fourth beats.

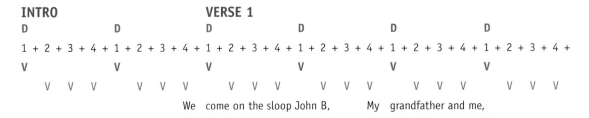

```
INTRO                           VERSE 1
D              D                D              D              D              D
1 + 2 + 3 + 4 + 1 + 2 + 3 + 4 + 1 + 2 + 3 + 4 + 1 + 2 + 3 + 4 + 1 + 2 + 3 + 4 + 1 + 2 + 3 + 4 +
V              V                V              V              V              V
   V  V  V        V  V  V          V  V  V        V  V  V        V  V  V        V  V  V
                                We   come on the sloop John B,     My   grandfather and me,
```

Try this pattern for the whole song. If it's hard for you to make a chord change, don't worry about strumming every beat, but keep time even when you don't strum the guitar. For example, look at the next phrase in the song:

```
D              D                A7             A7
1 + 2 + 3 + 4 + 1 + 2 + 3 + 4 + 1 + 2 + 3 + 4 + 1 + 2 + 3 + 4 +
V              V                V              V
   V  V  V        V  V  V          V  V  V        V  V  V
round    Nassau  town     we did  roam               Drinking all
```

If you need more time to switch chords, don't slow the tempo of the song by stalling after the fourth beat of the second bar. Instead, don't play the third and fourth beats of the second bar, and switch chords during that time.

```
D              D                A7             A7
1 + 2 + 3 + 4 + 1 + 2 + 3 + 4 + 1 + 2 + 3 + 4 + 1 + 2 + 3 + 4 +
V              V                V              V
   V  V  V           V   switch    V  V  V        V  V  V
round    Nassau  town     we did  roam               Drinking all
```

Remember, the song's time and tempo shouldn't stop for you. As your fretting hand gets faster, you can add those additional strums.

CHAPTER 11

The Capo and Barre Chords

Not all chords can be played as open chords. This chapter shows you how to play them using the barre chord technique. Barre chords enable you to take similar chord shapes and move them up and down the neck of the guitar.

Use a Capo

If you know only open chords, you may find that the chords don't match your vocal range when you try to sing as you play the guitar. A capo enables you to take the open chords you know and move them up and down the guitar neck.

WHAT A CAPO IS

A capo is a clamp with a hard rubber surface that presses against the strings of a particular fret. It's held in place by a spring mechanism or an elastic band. The effect is that the capo becomes a moveable nut, shortening the guitar's scale.

To use a capo, place it right behind the appropriate fret, but not on the fret itself. Make sure to lift it cleanly over the strings before you fasten it to the neck, or it may throw off your tuning.

HOW A CAPO WORKS

The capo makes chords sound higher by shortening the scale length of the guitar. It moves chords up the *chromatic scale*—a musical scale in which pitches are divided into 12 equidistant intervals. Each interval (the distance between two adjacent notes) is known as a half step. The notes of the chromatic scale are as follows:

C	C♯	D	D♯	E	F	F♯	G	G♯	A	A♯	B	C
	or		or			or		or		or		
	D♭		E♭			G♭		A♭		B♭		

For every fret the capo is placed on, that's how far the chord moves up the chromatic scale. For example, when you place the capo on the 1st fret, all your open chords move one half step up the chromatic scale. Playing a C chord with a capo on the 1st fret makes it sound like a C♯ or D♭ chord.

C	C♯	D	D♯	E	F	F♯	G	G♯	A	A♯	B	C
→	or		or			or		or		or		
	D♭		E♭			G♭		A♭		B♭		

If you move the capo to the 2nd fret and play the C chord again, the actual chord sound will be D, which is two half steps above C. The distance between two half steps is called a whole step.

C	C♯	D	D♯	E	F	F♯	G	G♯	A	A♯	B	C
	or	→	or			or		or		or		
	D♭		E♭			G♭		A♭		B♭		

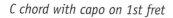

Capo goes here

Capo goes here

C chord with capo on 1st fret

C chord with capo on 2nd fret

Let's say you're playing a song that uses the D, G, and A chords, but it's a little too low to sing against. Try moving it up three steps by placing your capo on the 3rd fret. You're still playing the D, G, and A shapes, but the actual chords move up three half steps each.

D moves up to F (a).

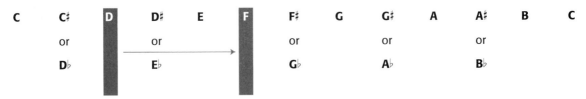

G moves up to A♯/B♭ (b).

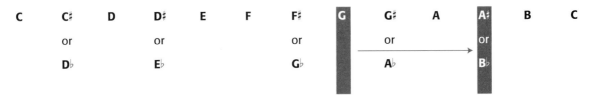

A moves up to C (c).

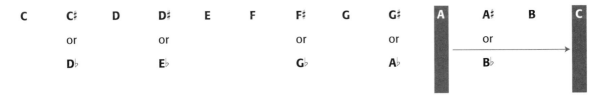

a   b   c

If the chords are still too low to sing against, continue moving the capo up. If the chords are too high, move the capo down. Most players don't place the capo higher than the 7th fret; if the chords are still too low to sing against, they'll choose to play the song in a different key.

The following tables illustrate what chords change to when you use a capo.

Capo on Fret	A	Am	A7	Am7
A, Am, A7, and Am7 Chords				
1	A♯/B♭	A♯m/B♭m	A♯7/B♭7	A♯m7/B♭m7
2	B	Bm	B7	Bm7
3	C	Cm	C7	Cm7
4	C♯/D♭	C♯m/D♭m	C♯7/D♭7	C♯m7/D♭m7
5	D	Dm	D7	Dm7
6	D♯/E♭	D♯m/E♭m	D♯7/E♭7	D♯m7/E♭m7
7	E	Em	E7	Em7
8	F	Fm	F7	Fm7

Capo on Fret	B7
B7 Chord	
1	C7
2	C♯7/D♭7
3	D7
4	D♯/E♭
5	E7
6	F7
7	F♯7/G♭7
8	G7

Capo on Fret	C	C7
C and C7 Chords		
1	C♯/D♭	C♯7/D♭7
2	D	D7
3	D♯/E♭	D♯7/E♭7
4	E	E7
5	F	F7
6	F♯/G♭	F♯7/G♭7
7	G	G7
8	G♯/A♭	G♯7/A♭7

Capo on Fret	E	Em	E7	Em7
E, E7, Em, and Em7 Chords				
1	F	Fm	F7	Fm7
2	F♯/G♭	F♯m/G♭m	F♯7/G♭7	F♯m7/G♭m7
3	G	Gm	G7	Gm7
4	G♯/A♭	G♯m/A♭m	G♯7/A♭7	G♯m7/A♭m7
5	A	Am	A7	Am7
6	A♯/B♭	A♯m/B♭m	A♯7/B♭7	A♯m7/B♭m7
7	B	Bm	B7	Bm7
8	C	Cm	C7	Cm7

Capo on Fret	G	G7
G and G7 Chords		
1	G♯/A♭	G♯7/A♭7
2	A	A7
3	A♯/B♭	A♯7/B♭7
4	B	B7
5	C	C7
6	C♯/D♭	C♯7/D♭7
7	D	D7
8	D♯/E♭	D♯7/E♭7

Let's use the capo to show what would happen to "Sloop John B." In the original key, the chords are:

D	D	D	D
come on the sloop John	B,	My grandfather and	me, A-
D	**D**	**A7**	**A7**
round Nassau	town we did	roam.	Drinking all
D	**D**	**G**	**G**
night,	Got into a	fight.	Well I
D	**A7**	**D**	**D**
feel so broke up,	I want to go	home.	So

If you decide that this song is slightly too low for you to sing, you can try putting the capo on the 2nd fret. Now every chord is one whole step or two chromatic steps higher. Playing the song with the original open chord shapes, the progression is now:

E	E	E	E
come on the sloop John	B,	My grandfather and	me, A-
E	**E**	**B7**	**B7**
round Nassau	town we did	roam.	Drinking all
E	**E**	**A**	**A**
night,	Got into a	fight.	Well I
E	**B7**	**E**	**E**
feel so broke up,	I want to go	home.	So

Barre Chord Technique

Playing a barre chord involves using your first finger as if it were a movable capo. Playing a barre chord involves a slightly different finger and wrist technique than the one you use to play ordinary chords.

You will need to learn to play barre chords because some major and minor chords can't be played as open chords.

How to Play a Barre Chord

Playing a barre chord involves laying the first finger across multiple strings. Let's concentrate on this technique before you play your first few barre chords.

1. Extend your first finger across the 2nd fret. This is called a 2nd fret barre. As with the other fingers, make sure that the first finger is directly behind the 2nd fret, but not on top of it.

You may want to roll your finger slightly to the outside edge (closer to your thumb). Doing so allows you to use the sharper edge of your finger and apply more direct pressure than the broader surface under your finger.

2 Although it's all right to let your thumb peek over the top of the neck for open chords, you'll need to reposition your thumb for barre chords. The thumb should be directly behind the first finger, which means that you drop the thumb lower behind the neck.

To accommodate this dropped-thumb position, you may also have to drop your wrist. If your wrist has a compressed or extreme angle, you may have to raise your arm. All of these issues can easily be resolved if you're playing in a proper, upright position.

TIP

Because playing a barre requires an unusual muscle configuration that is not exercised in everyday use, it can take a while to develop the muscles needed to maintain a proper barre. Be patient. Here's a trick you can use while your hand gains strength: Use your forearm muscles to pull your first finger toward your chest.

Your First Barre Chord: F

Fis often the first barre chord a beginner learns. Here, each chord is shown in three stages that you can move between as your muscles get used to the barre technique.

Don't feel as though you have to race to the full barre chord position. Take your time and move to the next level only when you're ready.

Beginner F Barre Chord

One set of barre chords moves E, Em, E7, and Em7 up and down the neck. You'll learn a beginner, intermediate, and full barre chord for F, so your hands will have time to develop the right muscles. Here's the E chord you learned earlier and the full F barre chord. As you'll notice, the second, third, and fourth fingers play the shape previously played by the first, second, and third fingers of the E chord. The extended first finger of the chord, known as the barre, essentially does the job of the nut in the E chord.

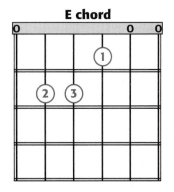

E chord

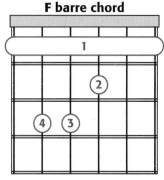

F barre chord

Here are the steps to finger the beginner F chord:

1 Place your first finger on the B (2nd) string, 1st fret.

2 Place your second finger on the G (3rd) string, 2nd fret.

3 Place your third finger on the D (4th) string, 3rd fret.

If you play the bottom four strings, you'll have a chord called Fmaj7 (pronounced "F major seventh").

4 The final step is to play what's called a *partial barre*. Flatten your first finger so that it covers the B (2nd) and High E (1st) strings at the 1st fret. You'll probably need to drop your thumb and wrist so you'll be able to support that first finger.

Apply pressure between your thumb and first finger. Now, if you play the bottom four strings, you've got an F chord! This is the *beginner* F barre chord shape.

Beginner F

F Barre Chord Shapes

Although you can use the beginner F chord now, let's look at the other F barre chord shapes.

INTERMEDIATE F BARRE CHORD

From the beginner shape, move your third finger from the D (4th) string, 3rd fret, to the A (5th) string, 3rd fret. Place your fourth finger on the D (4th) string, 3rd fret. Now you can play the lower five strings. This is the intermediate F barre chord shape.

Intermediate F

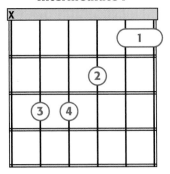

FULL F BARRE CHORD

To get the final shape, take the intermediate F chord shape and extend your first finger across all the strings. This is the *full* F barre chord shape.

Full F

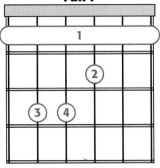

Related Barre Chords: F7, Fm, and Fm7

Once you've learned to play the F chord, you can play the other related barre chords of F7, Fm, and Fm7 with simple fingering variations.

F7 BARRE CHORD

If you go back to the F chord and lift up your fourth finger, you have the barre chord for F7. Notice that it's just an E7 chord using your first finger as a capo.

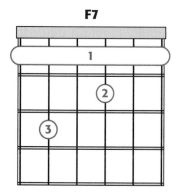

F7

Fm BARRE CHORD

If you go back to the F chord and lift up your second finger, you have the barre chord for Fm (pronounced "F minor"). Notice that it's just an Em chord, using your first finger as a capo.

Fm

F5 POWER CHORD

If you play only the bottom two (a) or three (b) strings, you have a modern chord hybrid called a *power chord*. It's not technically a chord because it's not a major or minor chord. The symbol for it is either F5 or Fno3 (pronounced "F no three"). I'll use the 5 designation. The power chord emerged in the late 1960s, when heavily distorted guitar tones came into vogue.

F5

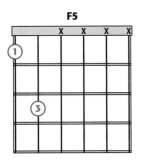

a

F5

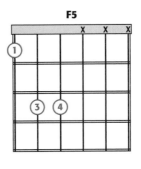

b

Fm7 BARRE CHORD

From this Fm shape, lift your fourth finger again, and you have the barre chord for Fm7 (pronounced "F minor seven"). Notice that it's just an Em7 chord using your first finger as a capo.

Fm7

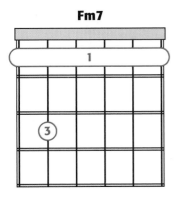

115

Moving Up and Down the Neck

Now that you've learned to play several types of barre chord shapes, you can move them up and down the neck in seemingly endless combinations.

More E-Shaped Chords

You can move the shapes you have just learned up and down the neck so that your first finger is on the 2nd fret. You've taken your E shape but moved its sound up two frets. You now have an F# or G♭ chord.

If you remove your fourth finger, you have an F#7 (pronounced "F sharp seven") chord, alternatively called a G♭7 (pronounced "G flat seven") chord. If you remove your second finger, you have an F#m (pronounced "F sharp minor") chord, alternatively called a G♭m (pronounced "G flat minor") chord. If you play the bottom two or three strings, you have an F#5 chord, alternatively called a G♭5 chord. If you remove your second and fourth fingers, you have an F#m7 (pronounced "F sharp minor seven") chord, alternatively called a G♭m7 (pronounced "G flat minor seven") chord.

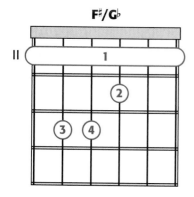

F#/G♭

F♯7/G♭7

II

F♯m/G♭m

II

F♯5/G♭5

II

117

F♯5/G♭5

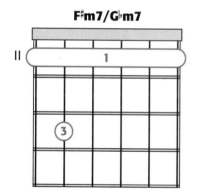

F♯m7/G♭m7

Here's the general chart for the E-shaped barre chords.

E-Shaped Barre Chords				
E	E7	Em	Em7	E5 (power chord)*

The open chord fingerings above correspond to the movable barre chords below.

First Finger Barre on Fret					
1	F	F7	Fm	Fm7	F5*
2	F#/Gb	F#7/Gb7	F#m/Gbm	F#m7/Gbm7	F#5/Gb5
3	G	G7	Gm	Gm7	G5
4	G#/Ab	G#7/Ab7	G#m/Abm	G#m7/Abm7	G#5/Ab5
5	A	A7	Am	Am7	A5
6	A#/Bb	A#7/Bb7	A#m/Bbm	A#m7/Bbm7	A#5/Bb5
7	B	B7	Bm	Bm7	B5
8	C	C7	Cm	Cm7	C5
9	C#/Db	C#7/Db7	C#m/Dbm	C#m7/Dbm7	C#5/Db5
10	D	D7	Dm	Dm7	D5
11	D#/Eb	D#7/Eb7	D#m/Ebm	D#m7/Ebm7	D#5/Eb5
12	E	E7	Em	Em7	E5

* You can play this power chord using two or three strings.

119

A-Shaped Chords

BEGINNER Bm BARRE CHORD

The other set of barre chords moves the A, Am, A7, and Am7 shapes up and down the neck. Start this series of chords by learning the Bm chord. As with the E family of barre chords, take your time and move to the next level of chords only when you're ready.

1 Put your first finger on the High E (1st) string, 2nd fret.

2 Place your second finger on the B (2nd) string, 3rd fret.

3 Place your third finger on the G (3rd) string, 4th fret. This is the beginner Bm barre chord shape.

If you play the three strings, you have a beginner Bm chord. Although you can start using the beginner Bm chord now, let's continue looking at the other shapes.

Beginner Bm

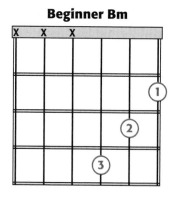

INTERMEDIATE Bm BARRE CHORD

From the beginner shape, move your third finger from the G (3rd) string, 4th fret, to the D (4th) string, 4th fret. Place your fourth finger on the G (3rd) string, 4th fret (where your third finger was). Now you can play the lower four strings. This is the *intermediate* Bm barre chord shape.

Intermediate Bm

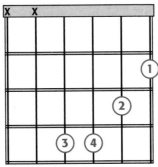

FULL Bm BARRE CHORD

To get the final shape, take the intermediate Bm chord shape and extend your first finger across all the strings. This is the *full* Bm barre chord shape.

Bm

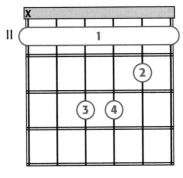

B, B7, AND Bm7 BARRE CHORDS

If you go back to the Bm chord shape; remove your second, third, and fourth fingers; and lay them down in the shape of an A chord; you have a B chord.

B

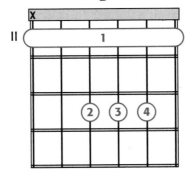

You can also play the shape by laying your third finger across the 2nd, 3rd, and 4th strings.

B

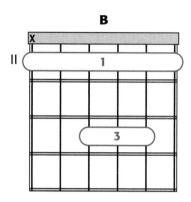

Go back to the Bm chord shape and remove your second, third, and fourth fingers again. Now place your third finger on the D (4th) string, 4th fret.

Now place your fourth finger on the B (2nd) string, 4th fret. You're placing an A7 shape above your finger, and it's now a B7 chord.

B7

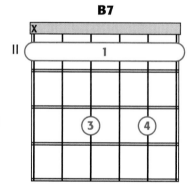

If you go back to the Bm chord and lift up your fourth finger, you have the barre chord for Bm7 (pronounced "B minor seven"). Notice that it's just an Am7 chord, using your first finger as a capo.

Bm7

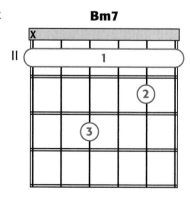

If you play only the bottom two (a) or three (b) strings, you have another set of power chords. The symbol for this chord is either B5 or Bno3 (pronounced "B no three"). I'll use the 5 designation.

The power chord can be used in two different settings:

B5

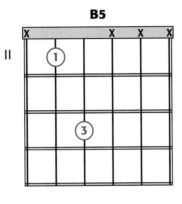

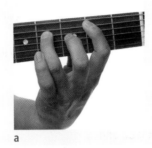

a

B5

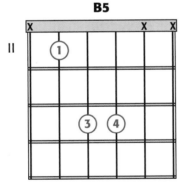

b

> **TIP**
>
> - If you find a major chord to be too "happy" but a minor chord to be too "sad," try using the power chord, which, because of its composition, is neither major nor minor.
> - If you're playing distorted electric guitar and certain notes sound wobbly or seem to vibrate oddly, try the power chord. Because of the inter-modulation of frequencies, distortion can make major and minor chords sound unstable. The power chord is less susceptible to this effect.

Here's the general chart for the A-shaped barre chords.

A-Shaped Barre Chords					
	A	A7	Am	Am7	A5 (power chord)*
	The open chord fingerings above correspond to the movable barre chords below.				
First Finger Barre on Fret					
1	A♯/B♭	A♯7/B♭7	A♯m/B♭m	A♯m7/B♭m7	A♯5/B♭5*
2	B	B7	Bm	Bm7	B5
3	C	C7	Cm	Cm7	C5
4	C♯/D♭	C♯7/D♭7	C♯m/D♭m	C♯m7/D♭m7	C♯m5/D♭m5
5	D	D7	Dm	Dm7	D5
6	D♯/E♭	D♯7/E♭7	D♯m/E♭m	D♯m7/E♭m7	D♯5/E♭5
7	E	E7	Em	Em7	E5
8	F	F7	Fm	Fm7	F5
9	F♯/G♭	F♯7/G♭7	F♯m/G♭m	F♯m7/G♭m7	F♯5/G♭5
10	G	G7	Gm	Gm7	G5
11	G♯/A♭	G♯7/A♭7	G♯m/A♭m	G♯m7/A♭m7	G♯5/A♭5
12	A	A7	Am	Am7	A5

* You can play this power chord using two or three strings.

CHAPTER 12

Arpeggios, Suspensions, and Bass Runs

You can make even the most basic chords sound more interesting by using arpeggios, suspensions, and bass runs. Arpeggios give a rolling feel from playing strings individually as opposed to playing them simultaneously in a strum. Suspensions create chordal tension and color, while bass runs connect and give chords momentum within a progression.

Arpeggios

To play an arpeggio, you play the strings of a chord one at a time, creating an interlocking pattern of sound. Think of the introduction to the Kinks' "Lola," right before the first verse, or the first section of Led Zeppelin's "Stairway to Heaven." All the guitar in the verses of the Police's "Every Breath You Take" and "Message in a Bottle" is done with arpeggios. Alternating between arpeggios and strummed chords can heighten a song's dynamics and contrast, such as the introduction of the Who's "Behind Blue Eyes" with its delicate arpeggios and slamming strummed bridge.

33 Play Your First Arpeggio

❶ Finger a D chord with your left hand.

❷ Place the bottom of your right hand close to the bridge. Doing so will create a pivot point on which you can anchor your hand. To move the pick from string to string, you have to rotate only your wrist, as opposed to moving your entire forearm.

3 Play the open D (4th) string with a down stroke.

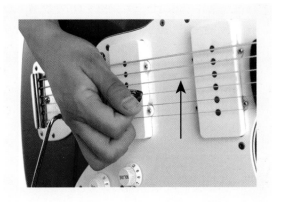

4 Continuing the down stroke, play the G (3rd) string, 2nd fret.

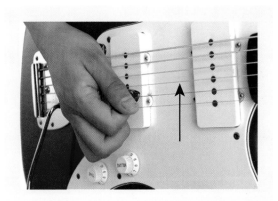

5 Continuing the down stroke, play the B (2nd) string, 3rd fret.

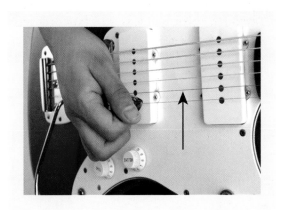

6 Reversing the pick motion to an up stroke, play the High E (1st) string, 2nd fret.

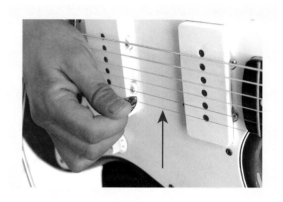

7 Continuing the up stroke, play the B (2nd) string, 3rd fret.

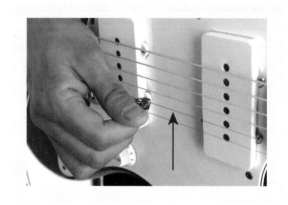

8 Continuing the up stroke, play the G (3rd) string, 2nd fret.

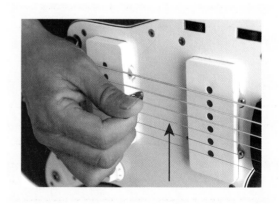

Now try the following arpeggios on different chords:

34 A

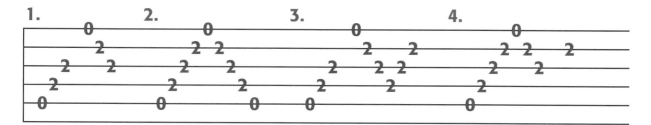

Am

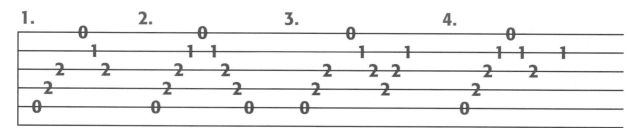

A7

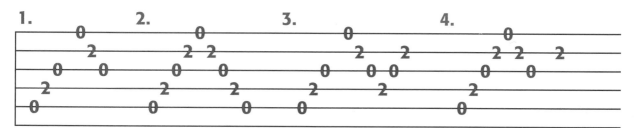

35 B7

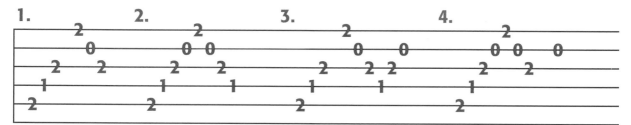

Arpeggios *(continued)*

Bm

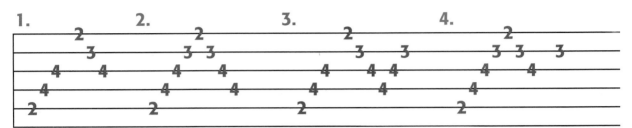

36 🎤 **C**

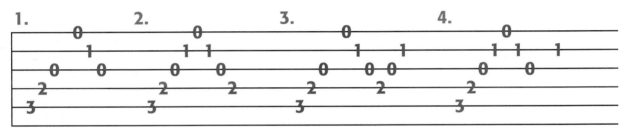

C7

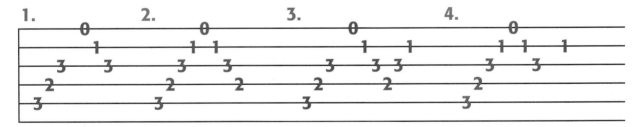

37 🎤 **D**

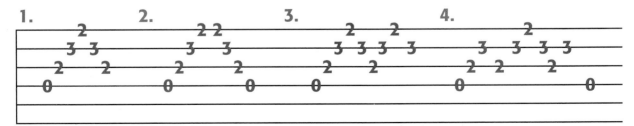

Dm

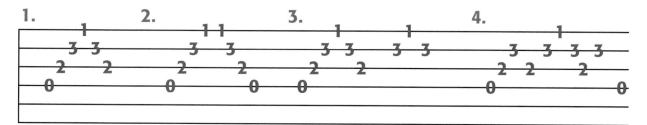

D7

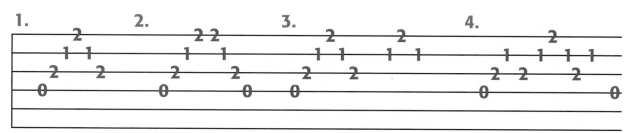

 38 **E**

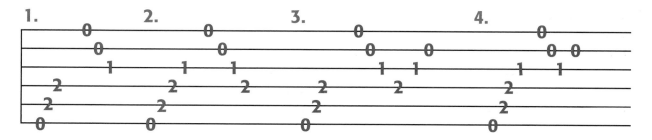

E7

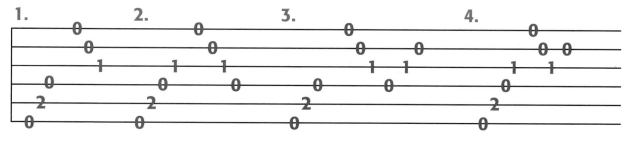

Em

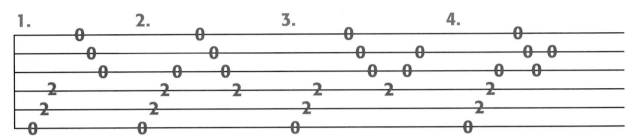

39 🎤 F (VERSION 1)

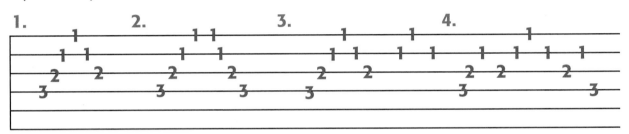

F (VERSION 2)

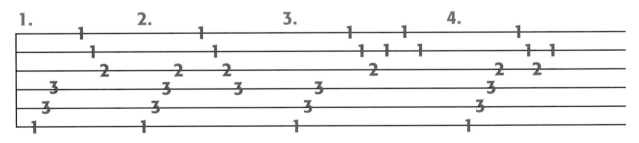

40 🎤 G

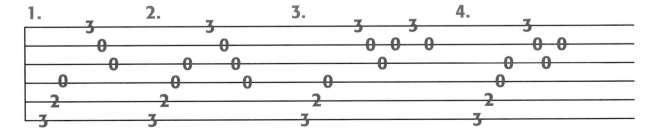

Suspensions add color to a chord by creating a floatier, unresolved sound, like the first chord of the Beatles' "A Hard Day's Night" or the Police's "Walking on the Moon." The top strings of regular chords and their suspensions can sound like mini-melodies when used together. Many of the suspensions can be made by removing or adding a finger. Check out the intros of the Beatles' "Ticket to Ride" and many Byrds tunes, such as "Feel a Whole Lot Better."

Play Your First Suspension

There are two similar chords, the terms of which are sometimes freely interchanged although they actually have different meanings. Add2, also commonly known as Add9, chords insert an extra note besides the regular tones. For example, the notes D, F#, and A comprise the notes of a D chord, whereas D, F#, A, and the ninth note of E. comprise a Dadd9 chord. Sus2 chords are similar, except the extra note replaces the middle note of the chord. For example, instead of the notes D, F#, and A that comprise the normal D chord, a Dsus2 is comprised of D, A, and the ninth note of E, which replaces the F#. For the purposes of this book I'll use the "sus" term to deal with both situations.

① Play a D chord, and you'll hear a chord sound that feels resolved. In other words, you can end a musical passage or song with this chord.

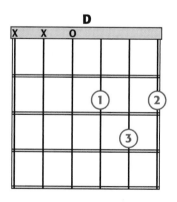

2 Now play the D chord, but without the second finger on the High E (1st) string, 2nd fret. This is called a Dsus2—a type of chord suspension. You may also see this chord called Dadd2 or Dadd9.

Dsus2

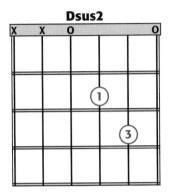

Notice that this chord seems to be floating up in the air. If you strum Dsus2 instead of D, the chord sounds more haunting or drifting. You can also use the Dsus2 chord between strums of a regular D chord, as shown at right. The slash marks stand for strums.

	D	D	Dsus2	D
	/	/	/	/
Beat	1	2	3	4

Now try another chord suspension. Go back to your original D chord and add your pinky to the High E (1st) string, 3rd fret. Now you have a suspension called Dsus4, which is commonly notated as Dsus.

Dsus4

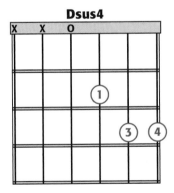

This chord has an even floatier feel than Dsus2. Again, you can use this chord as a substitute for D, but it is more commonly used before or between other D chords, as shown below. The first example shows four strums on Dsus4 followed by four strums on D. The second example shows two strums on D, two on Dsus4, two on Dsus2, and two on D.

	Dsus4				D			
	/	/	/	/	/	/	/	/
Beat	1	2	3	4	1	2	3	4
	D		Dsus4		Dsus2		D	
	/	/	/	/	/	/	/	/
Beat	1	2	3	4	1	2	3	4

Try placing suspensions anywhere you feel a chord needs more tension or harmonic contrast. Here's a chart of the easiest suspensions to add to your beginning chords. Names of notes and their fingerboard locations will be introduced in the next chapter.

Chord	sus2	sus4
A, Am, A7, Am7	B	D
C, C7	D	F
D, D7, DMaj7, Dm	E	G
E, E7, Em, Em7	F♯	A
F	G	B♭
G	A	C

NOTE 1: Whenever you add a sus2 to a seventh chord, you create a ninth chord.

    Example 1: A7 + sus2 = A9

    Example 2: Em7 + sus2 = Em9

NOTE 2: A sus4 chord is usually notated as just "sus" (Dsus4 = Dsus), but I've kept the 4 in the chart above to avoid confusion.

Suspension Chord Fingerings

Here are some common chords followed by suspension chord fingerings.

A

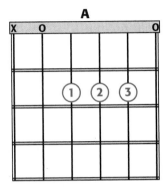

First finger on D (4th) string, 2nd fret

Second finger on G (3rd) string, 2nd fret

Third finger on B (2nd) string, 2nd fret

Asus2

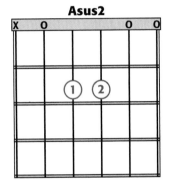

Remove third finger

Asus4

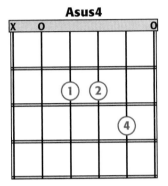

Add fourth finger to B (2nd) string, 3rd fret

A7

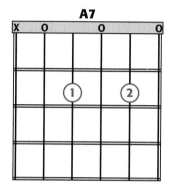

First finger on D (4th) string, 2nd fret

Second finger on B (2nd) string, 2nd fret

Am

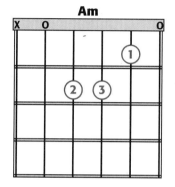

First finger on B (2nd) string, 1st fret

Second finger on D (4th) string, 2nd fret

Third finger on G (3rd) string, 2nd fret

Amsus2

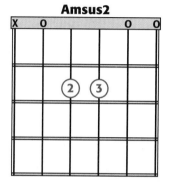

Remove first finger

This shape looks the same as Asus2.

Amsus4

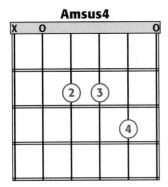

Am7

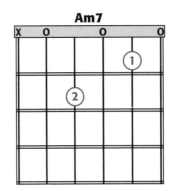

C

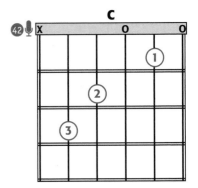

Add fourth finger to B (2nd) string, 3rd fret

This shape looks the same as Asus4.

First finger on B (2nd) string, 1st fret

Second finger on D (4th) string, 2nd fret

First finger on B (2nd) string, 1st fret

Second finger on D (4th) string, 2nd fret

Third finger on A (5th) string, 3rd fret

Csus2

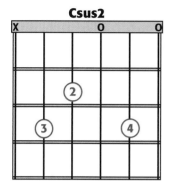

D

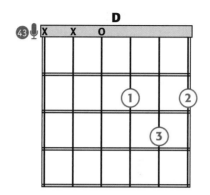

Dsus2

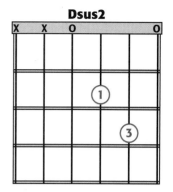

Add fourth finger on B (2nd) string, 3rd fret

First finger on G (3rd) string, 2nd fret

Second finger on High E (1st) string, 2nd fret

Third finger on B (2nd) string, 3rd fret

Remove second finger

139

Suspension Chord Fingerings *(continued)*

Dsus4

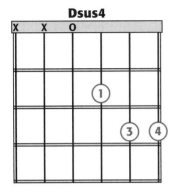

Add fourth finger on High E (1st) string, 3rd fret

D7sus4

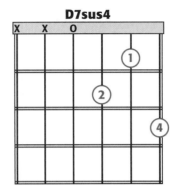

Add fourth finger on High E (1st) string, 3rd fret

Dmaj7

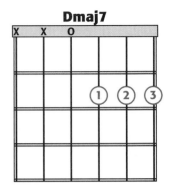

First finger on G (3rd) string, 2nd fret

Second finger on B (2nd) string, 2nd fret

Third finger on High E (1st) string, 2nd fret

Dm

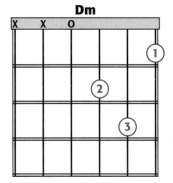

Dmadd2

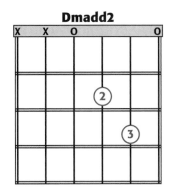

E

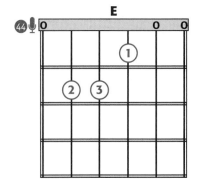

First finger on High E (1st) string, 1st fret

Second finger on G (3rd) string, 2nd fret

Third finger on B (2nd) string, 3rd fret

Remove first finger

This shape looks the same as Dadd2.

First finger on G (3rd) string, 1st fret

Second finger on A (5th) string, 2nd fret

Third finger on D (4th) string, 2nd fret

Esus4

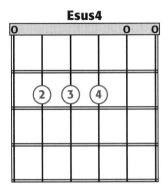

E7

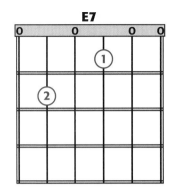

E7sus4

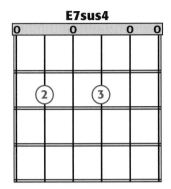

Add fourth finger on G (3rd) string, 2nd fret

First finger on G (3rd) string, 1st fret

Second finger on A (5th) string, 2nd fret

Add third finger on G (3rd) string, 2nd fret

Em

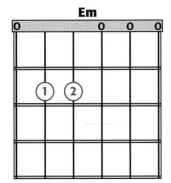

First finger on A (5th) string, 2nd fret

Second finger on D (4th) string, 2nd fret

Emsus2

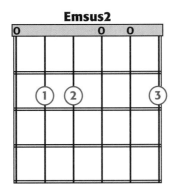

Add third finger on High E (1st) string, 2nd fret

Emsus4

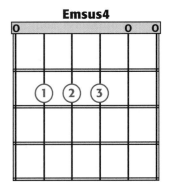

Add third finger on G (3rd) string, 2nd fret

Em7

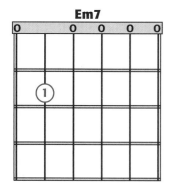

F

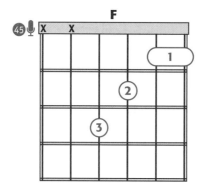

Fsus2

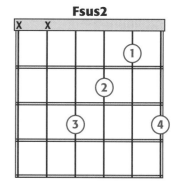

First finger on A (5th) string, 2nd fret

First finger on High E (1st) and B (2nd) strings, 1st fret

Second finger on G (3rd) string, 2nd fret

Third finger on D (4th) string, 3rd fret

Add fourth finger to High E (1st) string, 3rd fret, or remove second finger

Fsus4

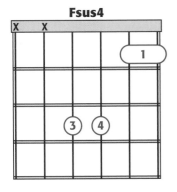

G

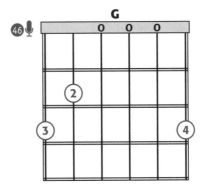

Gsus4

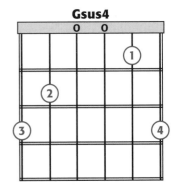

Add fourth finger to G (3rd) string, 3rd fret

Second finger on A (5th) string, 2nd fret

Third finger on Low E (6th) string, 3rd fret

Fourth finger on High E (1st) string, 3rd fret

Add first finger to B (2nd) string, 1st fret

Bass Runs

Some bass runs are single notes played before a chord is strummed (the Beatles' "Rocky Raccoon" intro). Other bass runs alternate between two notes (Johnny Cash's "I Walk the Line"). *Walking bass runs* walk up and down the scale between chords (the Beatles' "You've Got to Hide Your Love Away").

Play Your First Bass Run

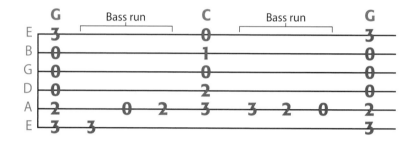

Here's an exercise you can do in the key of G, using the chords G and C. A great thing about this exercise is that you can play it forward and backward.

1 Strum the G chord.

2 Instead of immediately playing the C chord, first play a three-note bass run. The first note of the bass run is G, played on the 3rd fret of the Low E (6th) string.

③ The second note of the bass run is A, played on the open A (5th) string.

④ The last note of the bass run is B, played on the 2nd fret of the A (5th) string.

⑤ Finally, play the C chord.

Now play steps 4, 3, 2, and 1 again, and you have the entire run.

Single-Note Bass Patterns

The simplest bass runs involve hitting the root of the chords. The root is the lowest available note with the same name as the chord. Then hit the remaining higher-pitched strings and repeat.

Chords	Root String
A, A7, Am	5
B7	5
C, C7	5
D, D7, Dm	4
E, E7, Em	6
F	4/6
G	6

For example, on the A chord, hit the open A (5th) string.

 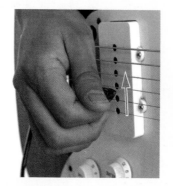 

TIP

If you slightly mute the root string with the heel of your hand close to the bridge, you can give the bass note a nice percussive thunk.

48 A

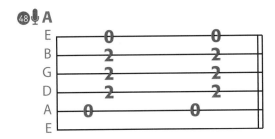

A7

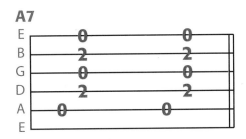

Am

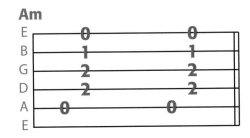

Am7

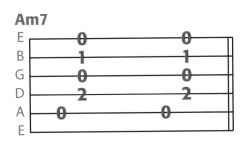

49 B7

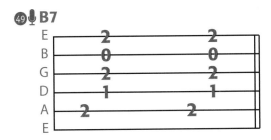

Bm

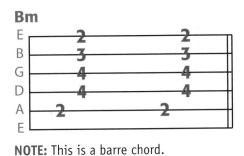

NOTE: This is a barre chord.

50 C

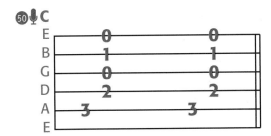

C7

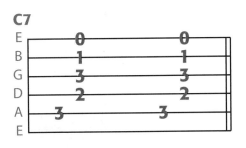

51 D

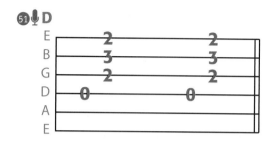

D7

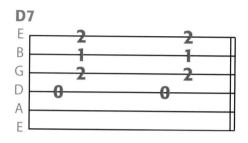

Dm

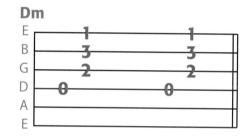

E

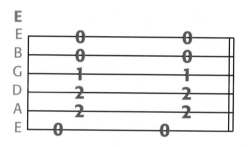

52 E7

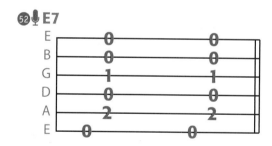

Em

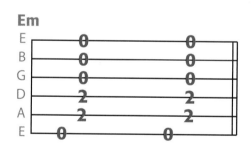

53 F (version 1)

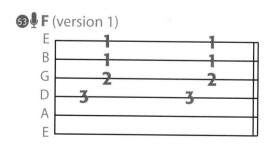

F (version 2)

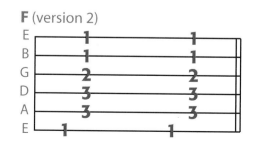

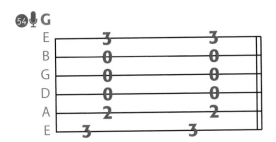

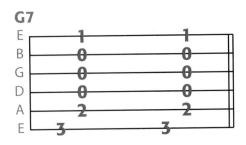

Alternate Bass Patterns

In an alternate bass run pattern, you alternate between the root string and the fifth of the chord. The fifth of the chord is four alphabetical letters up from the root. For instance, the fifth of the A or A minor chord is E, and the fifth of the C chord is G.

For example, on the A chord, hit the open A (5th) string first.

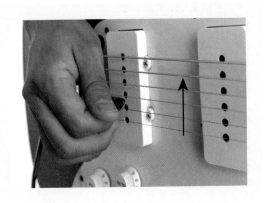

Then hit the remaining higher-pitched strings.

Then hit the fifth of the chord, E, by hitting the open E (6th) string.

Again, hit the remaining strings.

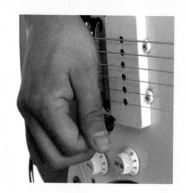

Chords	String with Root	Fifth of the Chord	String with Fifth of the Chord
A, A7, Am	5	E	6
B7	5	F♯	6 (move second fretting finger to 2nd fret)
C, C7	5	G	6 (move third fretting finger to 3rd fret)
D, D7, Dm	4	A	5
E, E7, Em	6	B	5
F	4 (ver 1)/6 (ver 2)	C	5 (you may have to move your third finger if you are playing the F (4th string)
G	6	D	4

55 A

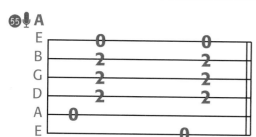

A7

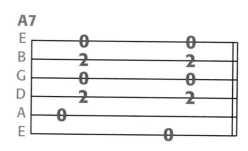

Am

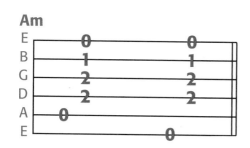

Am7

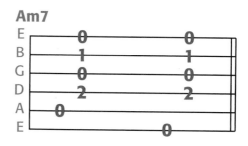

56 B7

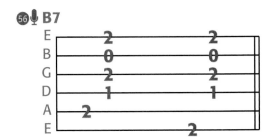

NOTE: You'll have to lift your second finger to move it back and forth from the A (5th) string to the Low E (6th) string.

Bm

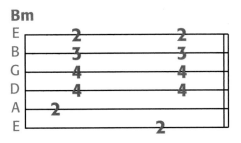

NOTE: This is a barre chord.

57 C

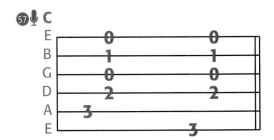

NOTE: You'll have to lift your third finger back and forth from the A (5th) string to the Low E (6th) string.

C7

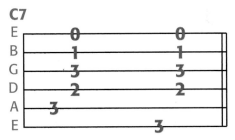

NOTE: You'll have to lift your third finger back and forth from the A (5th) string to the Low E (6th) string.

58 D

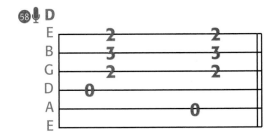

D7

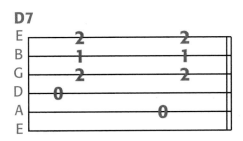

Dm

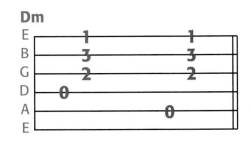

59 E

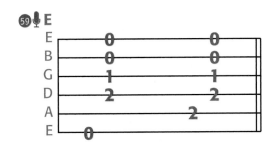

E7

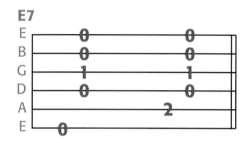

Em

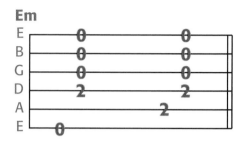

60 🎤 **F** (version 1)

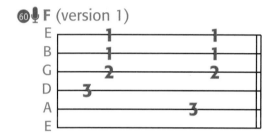

NOTE: You'll have to lift your third finger back and forth from the D (4th) string to the High E (1st) string.

F (version 2)

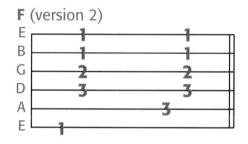

61 🎤 **G**

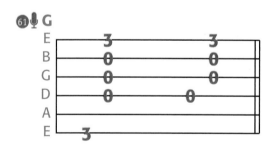

G7

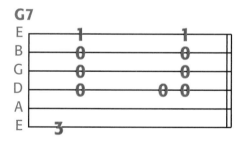

Walking Bass Runs

Walking bass runs involve a series of notes connecting two chords.

Let's do one in the key of A. We'll connect the A chord to the D chord and back to the A chord.

1 Play the root string of the A (5th) string.

2 Play the rest of the strings of the A chord.

155

③ Play the notes that will lead you to the D chord, B and C♯ on the A string.

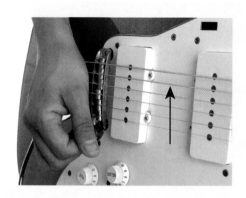

④ Finally, head back to the A chord by playing C♯ and B on the A string before playing the A string root and chord again.

WALKING BASS RUNS IN A

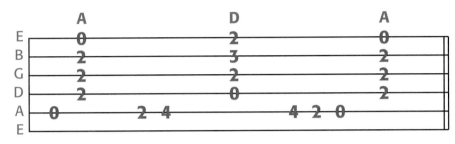

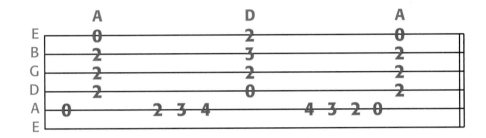

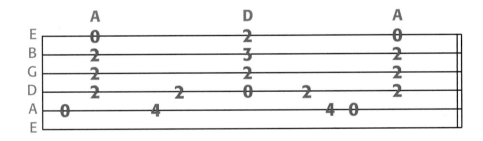

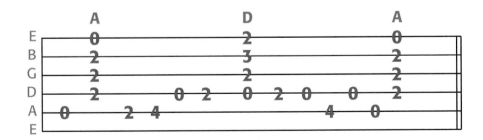

Bass Runs *(continued)*

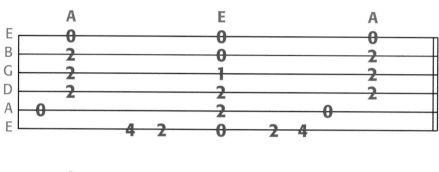

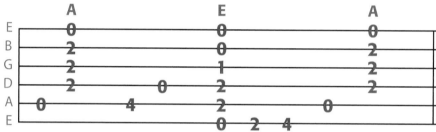

63 🎤 WALKING BASS RUNS IN C

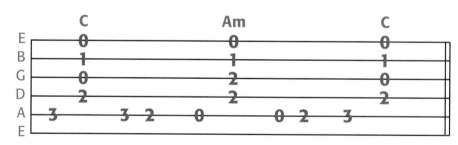

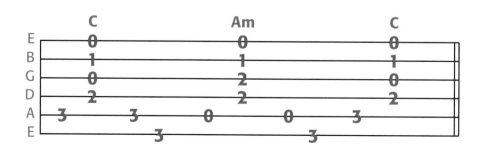

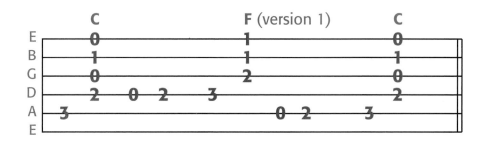

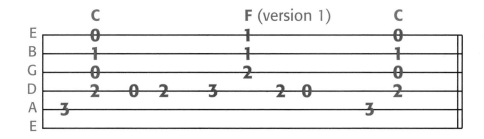

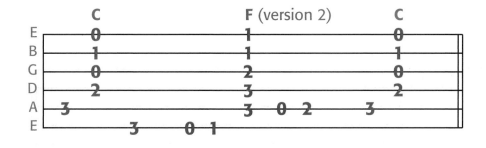

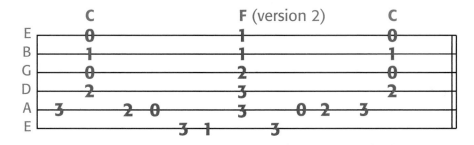

Bass Runs *(continued)*

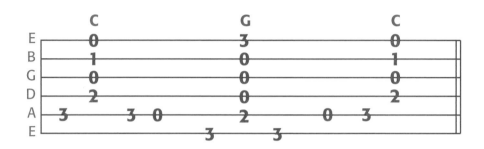

64 WALKING BASS RUNS IN D

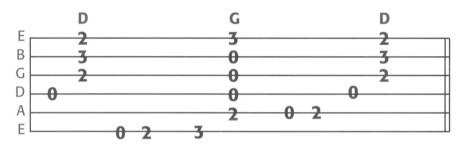

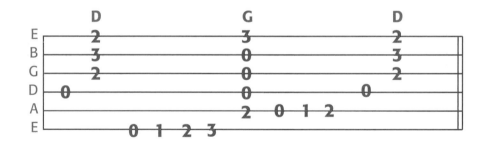

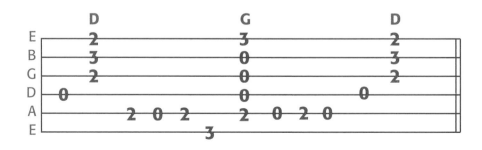

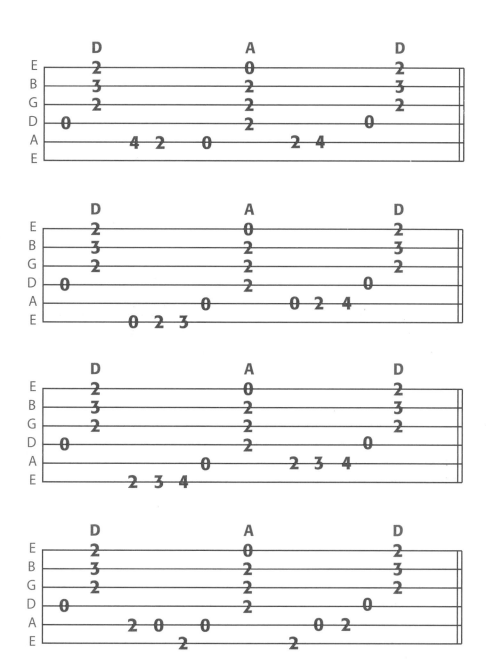

Bass Runs *(continued)*

65 🎤 **WALKING BASS RUNS IN E**

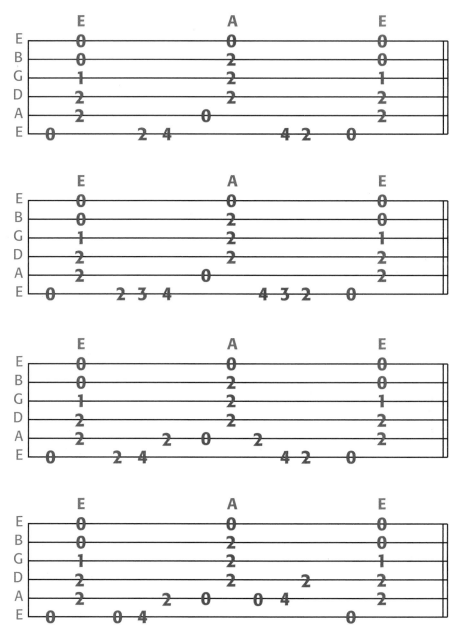

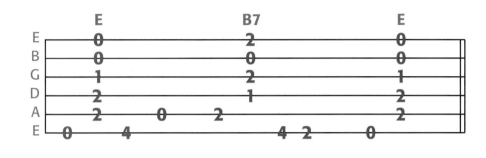

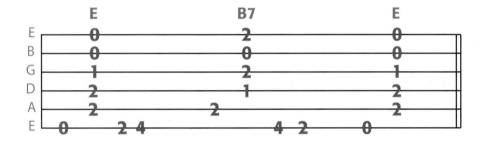

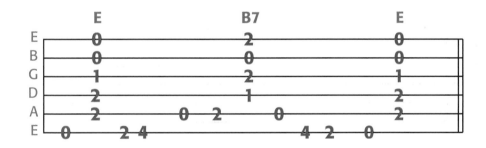

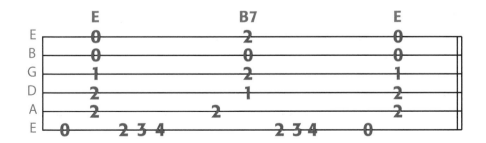

Bass Runs *(continued)*

66 Walking Bass Runs in G

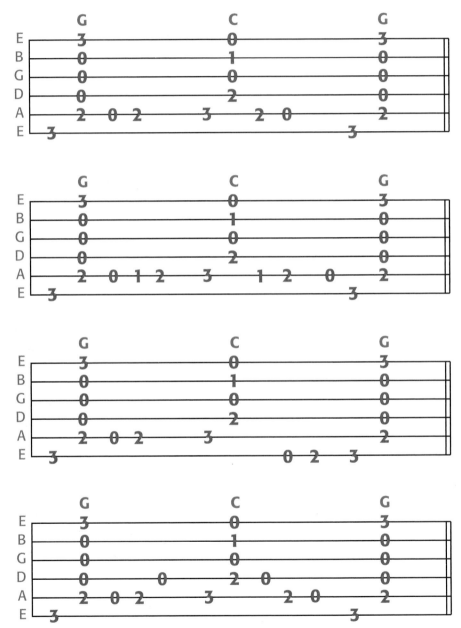

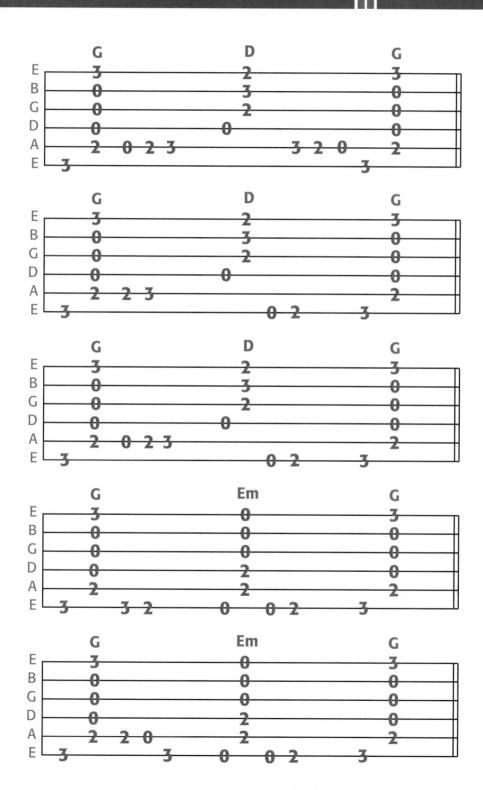

CHAPTER 13

Reading Music and Basic Theory

Reading tablature is quick and efficient—it tells you where on the guitar neck notes are played and which frets to play. It also allows for direction of guitar-specific techniques such as slides, hammer-ons, and pull-offs. However, tablature has no way of notating time, whether it is the duration of a note or rest, or where the music starts or stops in relation to the bar. You may think that reading staff notation is more difficult because of all the additional variables, but it is more rewarding and useful in the long run, especially as you learn more advanced melodies.

The Chromatic Scale

Western music assigns pitches to a 12-note scale, referred to as the *chromatic scale*. The interval between two consecutive chromatic notes (such as C and C♯) is referred to as a half step. Here are the notes of the chromatic scale, starting from C:

ENHARMONIC NOTES

Some of the notes on the chromatic scale notes have two names. For example, the note C♯ is the same as D♭. C♯ and D♭ are referred to as *enharmonic notes*. The enharmonic notes are:

C♯ = D♭   D♯ = E♭   F♯ = G♭   G♯ = A♭   A♯ = B♭

FIGURING OUT THE REST OF THE NOTES ON THE NECK

If you know the chromatic scale and the open notes of the guitar, you can figure out the rest of the notes on the neck.

On the High E (1st) string, the open string is obviously tuned to E. If you start up the frets using the chromatic scale, you get:

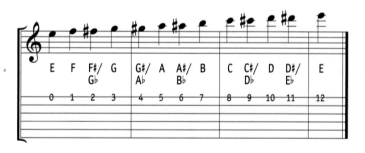

On the B (2nd) string:

On the G (3rd) string:

On the D (4th) string:

On the A (5th) string:

Finally, on the Low E (6th) string:

Here's a map of the entire fingerboard.

E	F	F♯/G♭	G	G♯/A♭	A	A♯/B♭	B	C	C♯/D♭	D	D♯/E♭
B	C	C♯/D♭	D	D♯/E♭	E	F	F♯/G♭	G	G♯/A♭	A	A♯/B♭
G	G♯/A♭	A	A♯/B♭	B	C	C♯/D♭	D	D♯/E♭	E	F	F♯/G♭
D	D♯/E♭	E	F	F♯/G♭	G	G♯/A♭	A	A♯/B♭	B	C	C♯/D♭
A	A♯/B♭	B	C	C♯/D♭	D	D♯/E♭	E	F	F♯/G♭	G	G♯/A♭
E	F	F♯/G♭	G	G♯/A♭	A	A♯/B♭	B	C	C♯/D♭	D	D♯/E♭
	I	II	III	IV	V	VI	VII	VIII	IX	X	XI

As a beginner guitarist, you should try to learn and memorize the first five frets of the guitar so that you can play basic melodies.

Scales *(continued)*

The Major Scale

The major scale is the most common scale in Western music. It is a seven-note scale (eight if you count the *octave,* the same note 12 half steps above the beginning note).

If you start on the E note, the E major scale comprises the notes E, F♯, G♯, A, B, C♯, and D♯. To play this scale across the High E (1st) string:

E	()	F♯	()	G♯	A	()	B	()	C♯	()	D♯	E
Open	1	2	3	4	5	6	7	8	9	10	11	12

If you count the number of half steps between the notes of the scale, you get the pattern 2 2 1 – 2 2 2 1.

	2		2		1		2		2		2		1	
E		F♯		G♯	A		B		C♯		D♯	E		
Open	1	2	3	4	5	6	7	8	9	10	11	12		

A whole step is two consecutive half steps, such as C to D. Therefore, you can describe a major scale in terms of half steps and whole steps: whole whole half – whole whole whole half.

	Whole		Whole		Half		Whole		Whole		Whole		Half	
E		F♯		G♯	A		B		C♯		D♯	E		
Open	1	2	3	4	5	6	7	8	9	10	11	12		

68 SCALES FOR COMMON KEYS

Here are the scales for the most common major keys for guitar:

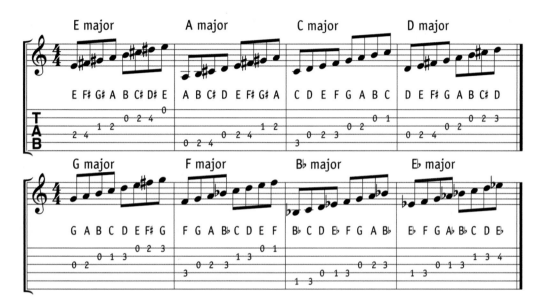

Scales *(continued)*

The Minor Scale

Minor scales typically sound darker and sadder than major scales, but have the same notes. The notes of the C major scale are C D E F G A B. If you restart the scale at A, you get the A minor scale. Its notes are A B C D E F G.

Because it has the same notes, A minor is known as the *relative minor scale* of C major. Notice that if you start on the 6th note of the major scale (in this case, A), you get the first note of the relative minor scale.

Major Scale	Notes	Relative Minor Scale	Notes
C major	C D E F G A B	A minor	A B C D E F G
D major	D E F♯ G A B C♯	B minor	B C♯ D E F♯ G A
E major	E F♯ G♯ A B C♯ D♯	C♯ minor	C♯ D♯ E F♯ G♯ A B
G major	G A B C D E F♯	E minor	E F♯ G A B C D
A major	A B C♯ D E F♯ G♯	F♯ minor	F♯ G♯ A B C♯ D E

A MINOR OPEN

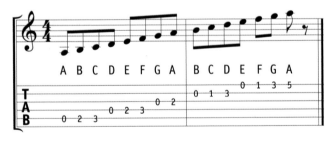

A MINOR MOVABLE

B MINOR OPEN

B MINOR MOVABLE

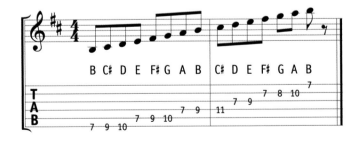

C♯ MINOR OPEN

C♯ MINOR MOVABLE

E MINOR OPEN

E MINOR MOVABLE

F♯ MINOR OPEN

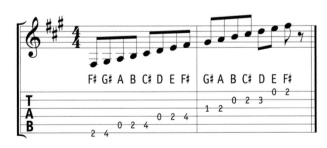

F♯ MINOR MOVABLE

The Treble Clef and Ledger Lines

The treble clef is the staff most commonly associated with the guitar. You read notes from left to right. The vertical position of a note indicates its pitch. The higher the note is on the staff, the higher it is in pitch.

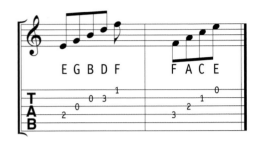

From bottom to top, the notes on the lines of the treble clef read E G B D F, commonly remembered by the mnemonic "**E**very **G**ood **B**oy **D**oes **F**ine." The middle line, B, corresponds to the pitch of the open B (2nd) string.

The spaces between the lines from bottom to top read **FACE**. The top space, E, corresponds to the pitch of the open High E (1st) string.

Notes that fall above or below the staff are notated with additional lines known as *ledger lines*. The highest line on the treble clef is F, which corresponds to the 1st fret on the High E (1st) string. The note that sits directly above that line is G, which corresponds to the 3rd fret on the High E (1st) string. The note above G is A, which corresponds to the 5th fret above the High E (1st) string. A ledger line is temporarily used above the F line. The note above A is B, which corresponds to the 7th fret above the High E (1st) string. This note sits above the first ledger line. Here are most of the notes above F.

The lowest line is E, which corresponds to the 2nd fret on the D (4th) string. The note that sits directly below that line is D, which corresponds to the open D (4th) string. The note below D is C, which corresponds to the 3rd fret above the A (5th) string. A ledger line is temporarily below the E line. The note below C is B, which corresponds to the 2nd fret above the A (5th) string. This note sits below the first ledger line. Here are all the notes below E.

Note and Rest Values

1+2+3+4+

1+2+   3+4+

WHOLE NOTES

A whole note represents four beats, with each beat representing four foot taps. A whole note is counted as "1 + 2 + 3 + 4 +" (or "one and two and three and four and"). The + symbol represents the halfway point of a beat, often referred to as the "and" of the beat, when your foot would come up.

HALF NOTES

A whole note is equal to two half notes. A half note represents two foot taps (up down up down). When two half notes are played in succession, the first half note is counted as "1 + 2 +" and the second is counted as "3 + 4 +."

1 + 2 + 3 + 4+

1 + 2+   3 + 4+

QUARTER NOTES

A half note is equal to two quarter notes. A quarter note represents one foot tap, up and down. Four consecutive quarter notes are counted as "1 +," "2 +," "3 +," and "4 +."

EIGHTH NOTES

A quarter note is equal to two eighth notes. Each eighth note is either a foot tap up or a foot tap down. Eight consecutive eighth notes would be counted as "1," "+," "2," "+," "3," "+," "4," and "+," respectively. When an eighth note occurs by itself, it looks like ♪. When they occur in pairs, their stems are connected, like ♫.

🎙️ DOTTED NOTES

Sometimes a note has a dot after it. The dot adds 50 percent of the symbol's time value. If a half note has a dot attached to it, it is referred to a dotted half note. Normally, a non-dotted half note would represent two beats counted as "1 + 2 +." Dotting that note adds an additional beat, counted "1 +." Adding those counts together, you would counted the dotted half-note as "1 + 2 + 3 +."

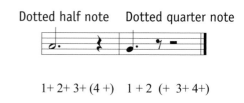

Dotted half note   Dotted quarter note

1+ 2+ 3+ (4 +)   1 + 2 (+ 3+ 4+)

RESTS

The same subdivision of time applies to rests, the counts of which are enclosed in parentheses in the examples at the right.

Whole note rest   Half note rest   Quarter note rest

(1+ 2+ 3+ 4+) 1+ 2+ (3+ 4 +) 1+   2+   3+ (4 +)

- A whole note rest represents four beats, each rest representing four foot taps, each up and down.

- A whole note rest is equal to two half note rests. A half note rest represents two foot taps, each up and down.

- A half note rest is equal to two quarter note rests. A quarter note rest represents one foot tap, up and down.

- A quarter note rest is equal to two eighth note rests. Each eighth note rest represents either a foot tap up or a foot tap down (see Chapter 9).

- An eighth note rest is equal to two sixteenth note rests. It is shown in the last measure after the dotted quarter note above.

Time Signatures

Time signature refers to how rhythm is divided in staff notation. The most common time signature is 4/4, or common time.

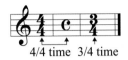

4/4 time 3/4 time

71 🎤 4/4 TIME

Music is broken down into units called *bars*. The top 4 in 4/4 time refers to four notes in each bar. The bottom 4 refers to those four notes being quarter notes. The combined time of four quarter notes can be divided by any combination of notes and rests, as long as it adds up to exactly four quarter notes. In other words, every bar must add up to "1 + 2 + 3 + 4 +."

72 🎤 3/4 TIME

The 3 in 3/4 time refers to three quarter notes in each bar. The combined time of three quarter notes can be divided by any combination of notes and rests, as long as it adds up to exactly three quarter notes. In other words, every bar must add up to "1 + 2 + 3 +."

Accidentals

A ccidentals are used to modify the pitches of notes.

SHARP SYMBOL

The sharp symbol (♯) before a note raises it one half step. A sharp before F, for example, turns the note to F♯. Every F, regardless of its octave, will be an F♯. This includes any F in the remainder of the bar. Any F after the bar will no longer be an F♯, unless a new ♯ symbol is used. The sharp symbol is rarely used before E, since the half step above it is F. The sharp symbol is also rarely used before B, since the half step above it is C.

F   F♯   F♯   F

FLAT SYMBOL

The flat symbol (♭) before a note lowers it one half step. A flat before B, for example, turns the note to B♭. Every B, regardless of its octave, will be a B♭. This includes any B in the remainder of the bar. Any B after the bar will no longer be a B♭, unless a new ♭ symbol is used. The flat symbol is rarely used before F since the half step below it is E. The flat symbol is also rarely used before C because the half step below it is B.

B   B♭   B♭   B

NATURAL SYMBOL

The natural symbol (♮) is used to negate the effect of a sharp or a flat, either in the key signature or from a sharp or flat that occurs earlier in the bar. If there is an F with a sharp, the pitch of the note will be F♯. A subsequent F in the same bar will also be an F♯, unless a natural sign is applied. (NOTE: The F in the next bar will not be an F♯, so a natural sign would not need to be applied.)

F   F♯   F   F   B   B♭   B   B

Key Signatures

As mentioned in "The Major Scale," several keys contain sharps or flats. A key signature allows you to specify the flats or sharps of a key next to the time signature, so you don't have to constantly read and write the accidentals. For example, the key of D has two sharps: D E F♯ G A B C♯.

In the time signature, you'll notice a sharp symbol in the F♯ and C♯ positions. Until another key signature is given, every F (in any octave) is an F♯, and every C is a C♯. If an F♯ needs to be an F temporarily in a specific bar, then you use a natural sign for that note.

Here are the key signatures for the following keys:

G MAJOR (OR E MINOR)

D MAJOR (OR B MINOR)

A MAJOR (OR F♯ MINOR)

E MAJOR (OR C♯ MINOR)

F MAJOR (OR D MINOR)

B♭ MAJOR (OR G MINOR)

E♭ MAJOR (OR C MINOR)

Now you can play these scales with their appropriate key signatures:

A MAJOR OPEN

A MAJOR MOVABLE

C MAJOR OPEN

C MAJOR MOVABLE

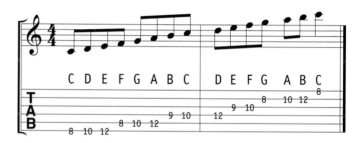

D MAJOR OPEN POSITION

D MAJOR MOVABLE

E MAJOR OPEN POSITION

E MAJOR MOVABLE

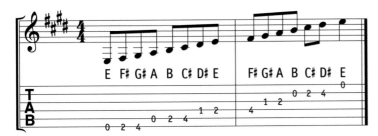

G MAJOR OPEN POSITION

G MAJOR MOVABLE

Here are other keys that use flats:

F MAJOR

B♭ MAJOR

E♭ MAJOR

F MAJOR OPEN

F MAJOR MOVABLE

B♭ MAJOR OPEN

B♭ MAJOR MOVABLE

E♭ MAJOR OPEN

E♭ MAJOR MOVABLE

TIP

When you're learning to read music, try learning the pitches of the notes first without worrying about time values. Then determine where the pitches should be played on the guitar. It's possible to play one note in several different places on the neck. The tone of the note may differ, though, based on the thickness of the string you choose. Finally, determine how long each note is played and when it starts. If you have trouble with a complex rhythm, try dividing the bar in half, like this:

1 + 2 + | 3 + 4 +

In other words, figure out what events occur in the first half of the bar (1 + 2 +) and what events occur in the second half of the bar (3 + 4 +).

Reading music and performing it simultaneously, known as sight-reading, takes lots of practice. Another way to practice reading music is to study the scores of songs you know so you can see how melodies in your head translate on a score.

CHAPTER 14

An Introduction to Soloing and Improvisation

Now that you've learned to recognize keys and the chords within a key, you can start playing solos and learning to improvise. This chapter shows you how to apply the pentatonic scale to the right key and how to create simple, effective melodies.

The Pentatonic Scale

The pentatonic scale is a simple five-note scale that has many applications across musical genres. This section shows you how to play it in movable shapes across the guitar.

74 🎙 Take a look at the set of notes to the right. This is a pentatonic scale because it has only five different notes: G, B, E, A, and D. This scale is known as the *E minor pentatonic* or *G major pentatonic scale.*

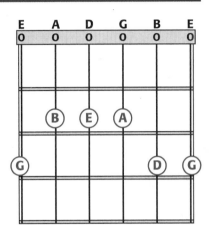

This boxlike shape is convenient because it's so easy to memorize. (Notice that this first scale uses all the open strings. This is not the case for all pentatonic scales.) This scale has two great applications. First, it can be used in the key of G Major or E minor to create a smooth, consonant sound. In other words, if the home chord is G, you can use the scale to play over these basic chords.

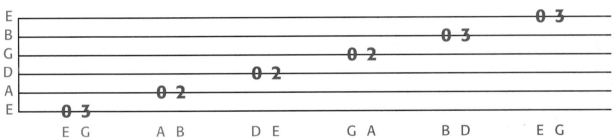

You can use the E minor pentatonic scale to play over chords in the key of G major.

Key	I	ii	iii	IV	V(7)	vi	♭VII	II(7)
G major	G	Am	Bm	C	D(7)	Em	F	A(7)
Key	i	III	iv	V	VI	VII	V(7)	
E minor	Em	G	Am	Bm	C	D	B(7)	

75 Second, you can shift the scale shape up three frets to get a bluesier sound over the key of G. Now your notes are G, B♭, C, D, and F.

This scale is called the *G minor pentatonic scale.*

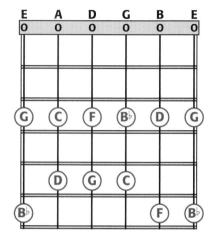

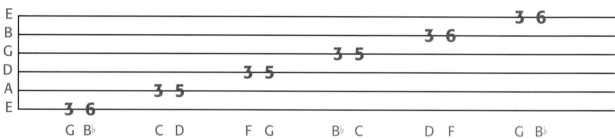

```
E                                                    3  6
B                                          3  6
G                                  3  5
D                          3  5
A                  3  5
E          3  6
        G  B♭      C  D      F  G      B♭  C      D  F      G  B♭
```

You can add one more note, called the "blue note," to create an even funkier, more dissonant sound. This scale is called the *blues scale.*

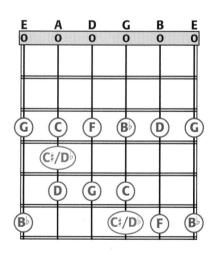

76 🎤 The blues scale is called a *movable scale* because it can be moved up or down depending on the key. Here is the *G blues scale:*

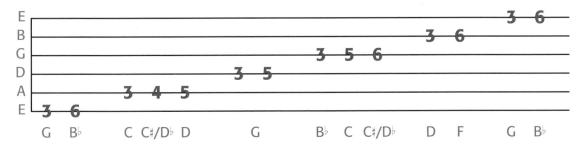

The table on the following page shows you which chords and pentatonic scales can be used on each major key. For example, if you're in the key of C, the most likely chords are C, Dm, Em, F, G, and Am. You can also use B♭ and E♭ for blues or heavier rock, and D or D7 for pop.

There are three basic scale choices available in C. One is the *major pentatonic scale,* where your first finger is on the 5th fret, your third finger plays the 7th fret, and your fourth finger plays the 8th fret. This scale over these chords gives a melodic, consonant sound. You may hear musicians refer to it as sounding "in."

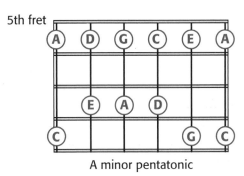

A minor pentatonic

The second is the *minor pentatonic scale,* where your first finger is on the 8th fret, your third finger plays the 10th fret, and your fourth finger plays the 11th fret. This scale over these chords gives a darker, dissonant sound. You may hear musicians refer to it as sounding "out."

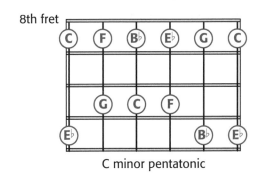

C minor pentatonic

The third is the *C blues scale,* which looks like the minor pentatonic scale, with an extra note called the "blue note" of F♯/G♭, which makes the scale sound even darker and more dissonant.

Again, this table shows which chords and pentatonic scales can be used on each major key.

8th fret

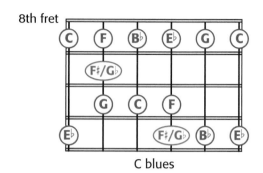

C blues

Key	I	ii	iii	IV	V(7)	vi	♭VII	♭III	II(7)	Pentatonic Scale Starts on Fret	
										Major	Minor/ Blues
C major	C	Dm	Em	F	G(7)	Am	B♭	E♭	D(7)	5	8
D major	D	Em	F♯m	G	A(7)	Bm	C	F	E(7)	7	10
E major	E	F♯m	G♯m	A	B(7)	C♯m	D	G	F♯(7)	9	12 or open
F major	F	Gm	Am	B♭	C(7)	Dm	E♭	A♭	G(7)	10	1 or 13
G major	G	Am	Bm	C	D(7)	Em	F	B♭	A(7)	12 or open	3
A major	A	Bm	C♯m	D	E(7)	F♯m	G	C	B(7)	2	5

The table on the following page shows which chords and pentatonic scales can be used on each minor key. For example, if you're in the key of Am, the most likely chords are Am, C, Dm, Em, E7, F, and G.

Two scales are commonly used. The first is the minor pentatonic scale, where your first finger is on the 5th fret, your third finger plays the 7th fret, and your fourth finger plays the 8th fret. This scale over these chords gives a minor chord a melodic, consonant sound. Notice that we used this same scale over the key of C Major. The two keys are very closely related. In fact, they are referred to as *relative major and minor keys.*

5th fret

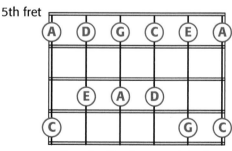

C major/A minor pentatonic

The second is the *A blues scale,* which looks like the minor pentatonic scale, with an extra note called the "blue note" of D♯/E♭, which makes the scale even darker and more dissonant.

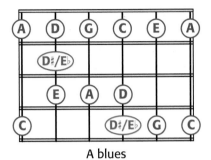

A blues

Key	i	III	iv	v	VI	VII	V(7)	Pentatonic Scale Starts on Fret For Both Minor and Blues
A minor	Am	C	Dm	Em	F	G	E(7)	5
B minor	Bm	D	Em	F♯m	G	A	F♯(7)	7
C♯ minor	C♯m	E	F♯m	G♯m	A	B	G♯(7)	9
D minor	Dm	F	Gm	Am	B♭	C	A(7)	10
E minor	Em	G	Am	Bm	C	D	B(7)	12 or open
F♯ minor	F♯m	A	Bm	C♯m	D	E	C♯(7)	2

Simple Solos

Now try using this scale information in these simple solo phrases.

A MAJOR PENTATONIC

E F# A B A   E F# A B C#   F# A B C# C#   F# A B C# A   F# A B C# E

A B C# E   A B C# E C#   E F# E F# A B A   E F# A B F# A B C#

77 🎤 A MINOR PENTATONIC

Simple Solos *(continued)*

77 🎤 A BLUES

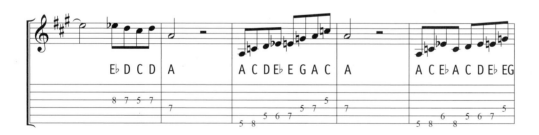

78 C MAJOR PENTATONIC

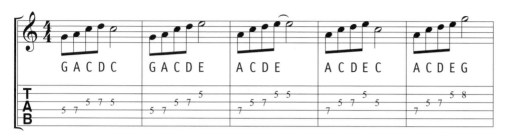

78 C MINOR PENTATONIC

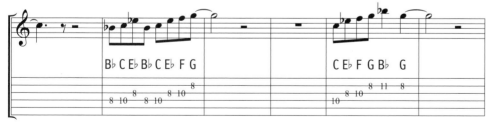

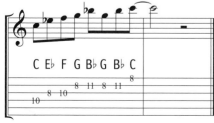

78 🎤 C BLUES

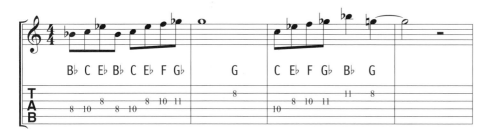

Bb C Eb Bb C Eb F Gb   G   C Eb F Gb Bb G

C Eb F Gb G Gb Bb C   Eb C Bb C G Gb F Eb   C   Eb C Bb C Bb G

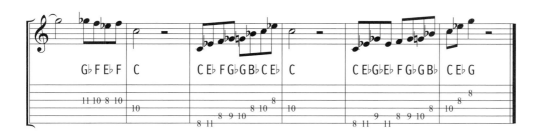

Gb F Eb F   C   C Eb F Gb G Bb C Eb   C   C Eb Gb Eb F Gb G Bb   C Eb G

79 🎤 **D MAJOR PENTATONIC**

A B D E D   A B D E F#   B D E F#   B D E F# D   B D E F# A

D E F# A   D E F# A F#   A B A B D E D

79 🎤 **D MINOR PENTATONIC**

C D F C D   C D F C D C D F   C D   C D F C D F C D

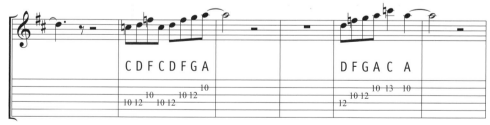

C D F C D F G A   D F G A C A

D F G A C A C D

Simple Solos *(continued)*

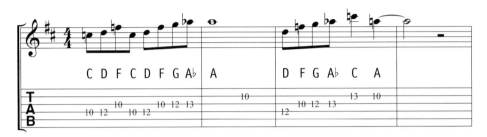

C D F C D F G A♭   A   D F G A♭   C   A

D F G A♭ A A C D   F D C D A A♭ G F   D   F D C D C A

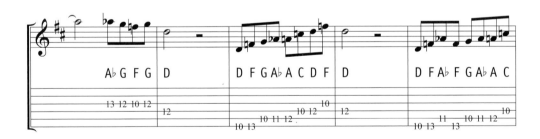

A♭ G F G   D   D F G A♭ A C D F   D   D F A♭ F G A♭ A C

D F A

196

80 🎤 E MAJOR PENTATONIC

B C♯ E F♯ E   B C♯ E F♯ G♯   C♯ E F♯ G♯   C♯ E F♯ G♯ E

C♯ E F♯ G♯ B   E F♯ G♯ B   E F♯ G♯ B G♯   B C♯ B C♯ E F♯ E

B C♯ E F♯ C♯ E F♯ G♯

Simple Solos *(continued)*

80 🎤 E MINOR PENTATONIC

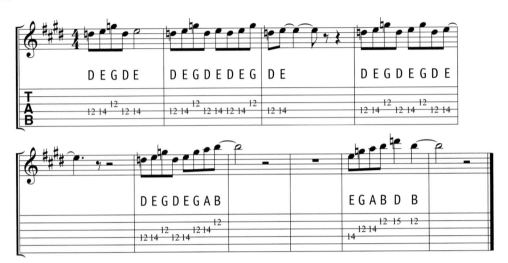

80 🎤 E BLUES

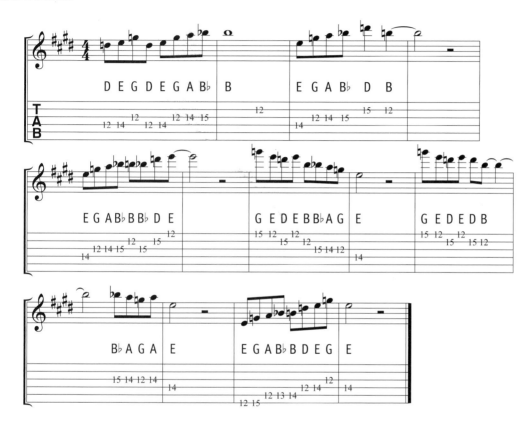

81 🎤 G MAJOR PENTATONIC

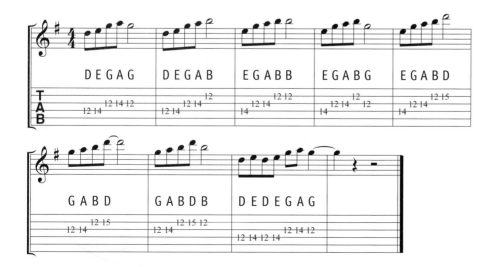

81 G MINOR PENTATONIC

81 G BLUES

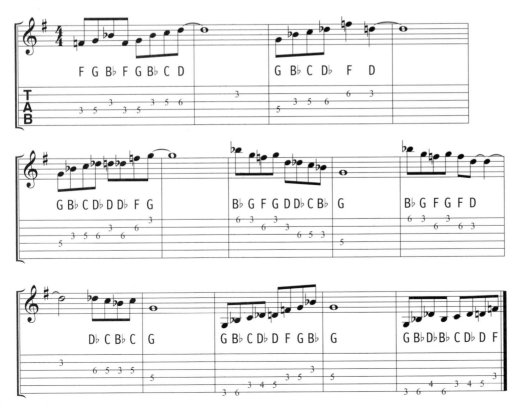

CHAPTER 15

Advanced Techniques

You've learned the basics of improvising; now try some different techniques in your solos. Slides, pull-offs and hammer-ons, and vibrato and string bending can all add more personality to your playing.

Slides

Sliding your finger from note to note gives your playing a more violin-like, liquid sound. It can make your guitar sound less percussive and more melodic.

Play a Slide

Instead of using different fingers of your fretting hand to play different notes, you can slide your finger from note to note on the same string. Here's one way of playing these two notes:

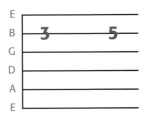

Your first finger plays the D note on the 3rd fret of the B (2nd) string (a), and your third finger plays the E note on the 5th fret of the B (2nd) string (b). You pick both strings individually.

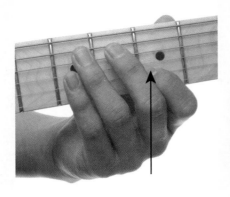

a

b

Now try this version:

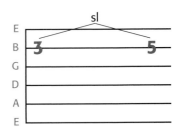

In this example, you pick only the D note on the 3rd fret of the B (2nd) string and then slide your first finger to the 5th fret of the B (2nd) string. The *sl* indicates that you slide between the 3rd (a) and 5th (b) frets and pick only the first note.

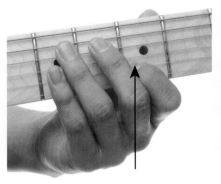

a

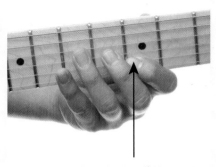

b

To make sure the sound doesn't fade away before you get to the 5th fret, use sufficient downward pressure on the string. You may also want to pick the first note closer to the bridge to get sufficient punch in the pick stroke.

TIP

You can use slides between notes if a phrase sounds too stiff or percussive. Sliding can give a guitar melody a more vocal, singing quality. Playing several slides on the same string can also give the guitar a more tonally consistent sound, since every string has a slightly different tone quality.

Here's a longer passage involving multiple slides up and down the neck.

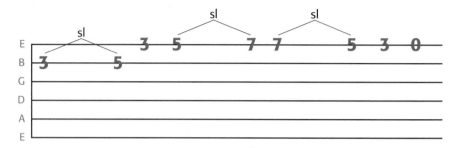

Pick 3rd fret of B (2nd) string

Slide third finger to 3rd fret of High E (1st) string

Pick 3rd fret of High E (1st) string

Pick 5th fret of High E (1st) string

Slide to 7th fret of High E (1st) string

Pull-Offs and Hammer-Ons

L ike slides, pull-offs and hammer-ons produce a fluid sound. The fretting hand creates the sound on the string with some additional force. This makes some passages easier to play because you don't have to pick as many notes.

Pull-Off to Open Strings

Let's try a pull-off. Place your third finger on the 3rd fret of the High E (1st) string (a). Without using your picking hand, pluck the High E string with your third finger by pulling it toward the floor (b). You are essentially fingerpicking by using a finger on your fretting hand. The symbol *po* on the tablature refers to a pull-off.

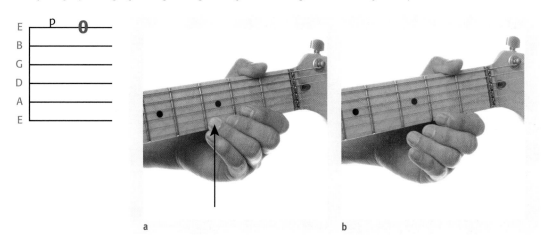

```
E ┌─── P ─── 0 ───
B │
G │
D │
A │
E └─────────────────
```

a   b

Now use your picking hand to play the note on the G (3rd) string, and again pull-off to the open string. Pick the 3rd fret of the High E (1st) string (c). Then pull off with your third finger (d).

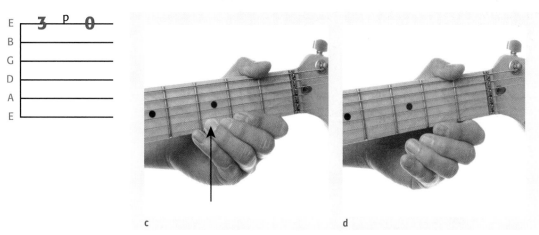

```
E ┌── 3 ── P ── 0 ──
B │
G │
D │
A │
E └─────────────────
```

c   d

Try a series of pull-offs on the same string, but pull off from the 3rd fret, then the 5th, 7th, and finally back on the 5th, all going to the open string.

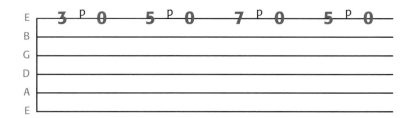

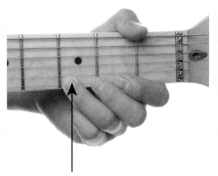

Pick 3rd fret of High E (1st) string

Pull off with third finger

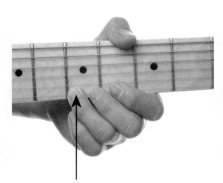

Pick 5th fret of High E (1st) string

Pull off with third finger

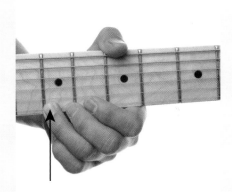

Pick 7th fret of High E (1st) string

Pull off with third finger

Pick 5th fret of High E (1st) string

Pull off with third finger

Pull-Off to Fretted Notes

You can also pull-off to other fretted notes, not just to open strings. In this example, the fourth finger pulls-off after the note on the 8th fret is picked. However, the first finger is placed on the 5th fret before the pull-off.

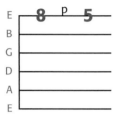

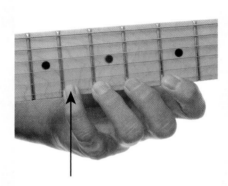

Pick 8th fret of High E (1st) string

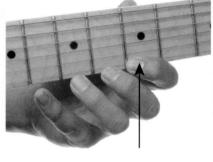

Pull off with fourth finger; string rings to 5th fret of High E (1st) string

Now let's try a series of pull-offs that go from the High E (1st) string, to the B (2nd) string, and finally to the G (3rd) string.

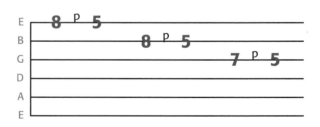

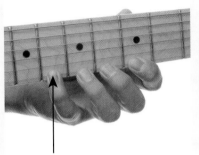

Pick 8th fret of High E (1st) string

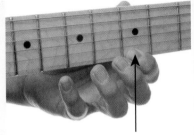

Pull off with fourth finger; string rings
to 5th fret

Pick 8th fret of B (2nd) string

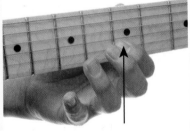

Pull off with fourth finger; string rings
to 5th fret

Pick 7th fret of G (3rd) string

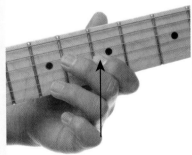

Pull off with third finger; string rings
to 5th fret

Play a Hammer-On

A hammer-on is the opposite of a pull-off. Pick the open High E (1st) string. Then, without using your picking hand, quickly and forcefully bring the third finger of your fretting hand down on the 3rd fret of the High E string. The force of your third finger, along with the momentum of the first picked note, should be enough to make the second note ring. The *h* in the tablature refers to the hammer-on.

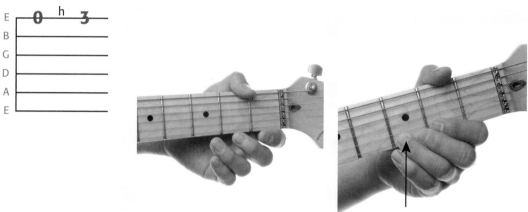

Pick open High E (1st) string

Hammer-on with third finger to 3rd fret

Now try a series of hammer-ons on the same string, all starting from the open string.

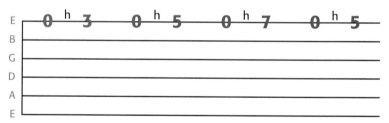

Pick open High E (1st) string

Hammer on to 3rd fret of High E (1st) string

Pick open High E (1st) string

Hammer-on to 5th fret of High E (1st) string

Pick open High E (1st) string

Hammer-on to 7th fret of High E (1st) string

Pick open High E (1st) string

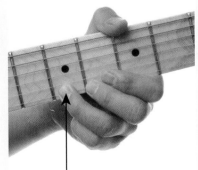

Hammer-on to 5th fret of High E (1st) string

The hammer-on and the pull-off can be used together to create a seamless, violin-like sound.

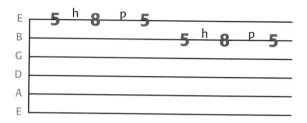

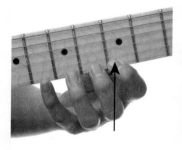

Pick 5th fret of High E (1st) string

Hammer on to 8th fret of High E (1st) string

Pull off to 5th fret of High E (1st) string

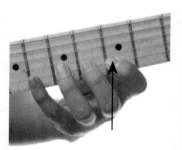

Pick 5th fret of B (2nd) string

Hammer on to 8th fret of B (2nd) string

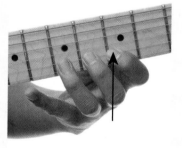

Pull off to 5th fret of B (2nd) string

Vibrato

To give a guitar note a vocal quality like a human singing voice, you use a technique known as vibrato, where the string is moved slightly back and forth to create a modulation of pitch. There are two basic types of vibrato: classical and vertical.

Classical Vibrato

For classical vibrato, you move a left-hand fingertip back and forth along the string length, causing the string to tighten and loosen slightly, which in turn causes the pitch to both rise above and fall below the original note. Classical vibrato is easier to apply to nylon-string guitars than to steel-string or electric guitars because the nylon-string tension is lower.

1 Place your left fingertip directly behind the fret of the note to be played and strike the string with your right hand.

2 Slowly rock and rotate your fingertip toward the fret. Doing so causes the string to slacken slightly and the pitch to drop.

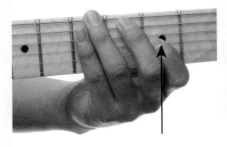

1

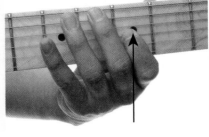

2

3 Slowly rock and rotate your fingertip away from the fret (see photo). Doing so causes the string to tighten slightly and the pitch to rise.

Move your fingertip back and forth at a faster tempo. The faster you move it, the quicker the vibrato. As the note fades, slow the tempo of the vibrato until your fingertip is in its original position.

3

Vertical Vibrato

For vertical vibrato, you move the string back and forth parallel to the frets. This type of vibrato is used in popular guitar styles, such as blues and rock. The pitch only rises in comparison to the original note. Here's an example using the third finger.

❶ Place the third fingertip of your left hand directly behind the fret of the note to be played. Place the first and second fingertips directly behind the third fingertip to lend extra muscle support. Place your thumb above the neck to be used as a fulcrum point, and strike the string with your right hand.

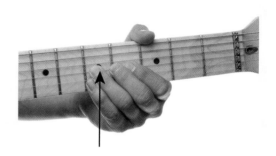

❷ Slowly push your third finger toward your thumb, using your first two fingers to help. Doing so causes the string to tighten slightly and the pitch to rise. When you relax your fingers, the string pulls to its starting position and the pitch returns to the starting pitch.

❸ Slowly pull your third finger away from your thumb, using your first two fingers to help pull (see photo). Doing so causes the string to tighten slightly and the pitch to rise. When you relax your fingers, the string pulls to its starting position and the pitch returns to the starting pitch.

Move your fingertip back and forth again, pushing and pulling faster this time. The faster you move your fingertip, the quicker the vibrato. As the note fades, slow the tempo of the vibrato until your fingertip is in its original position.

87 🎤 String Bending

The vertical vibrato technique (see the previous section) can also be used for string bending, where you move to a different note. String bending alters the pitch more radically. It's commonly used in rock, blues, and country music. Bend slowly when you start so you can make sure you're accurately hitting your target pitch.

---

❶ Play these two notes.

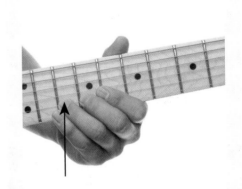

❷ Now, instead of playing the two notes separately, play the note at the 10th fret and then bend it up to the 11th. Make sure that the pitch of the bent note is the same as the 11th fret note. The *b* in the tablature refers to a bend.

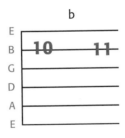

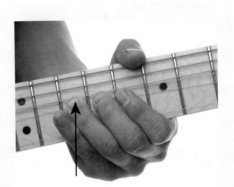

Bending involves first pressing down on the string with the fretting finger, then pushing the string up or down across the fingerboard to change the pitch. Try bending the E (1st), B (2nd), and G (3rd) finger up (i.e. toward your face, and bending the D (4th), A (5th), and E (6th) strings down (i.e. toward your feet).

You can also try bending two frets.
First play these notes:

Then try bending the 10th fret up to
the pitch of the 12th.

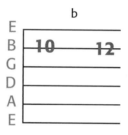

Once you reach your destination pitch, as shown here,
you can also apply vibrato, but be patient; these techniques involve specific muscle strength and memory.

88 Tremolo Bar

The tremolo bar, or whammy bar, is a movable bridge with springs that mount to the body of the guitar. It can create more radical pitch changes than regular finger vibrato can.

When the bar is depressed, the strings are detuned and the pitches go flat.

When the bar is raised, the strings are tightened and the pitches go sharp.

If you rock the bar back and forth, you can create either gentle vibrato or more intense wobbling effects.

Harmonics

H armonics are a bell-like sound created when the string is struck at certain division points while being touched lightly.

Natural Harmonics

If you lightly touch a string directly above the 12th fret while you pluck the string (a), it will ring an octave above the open string's pitch.

If you touch the string above the 7th fret (b), you'll hear a note an octave and seven chromatic steps above the open string, or B.

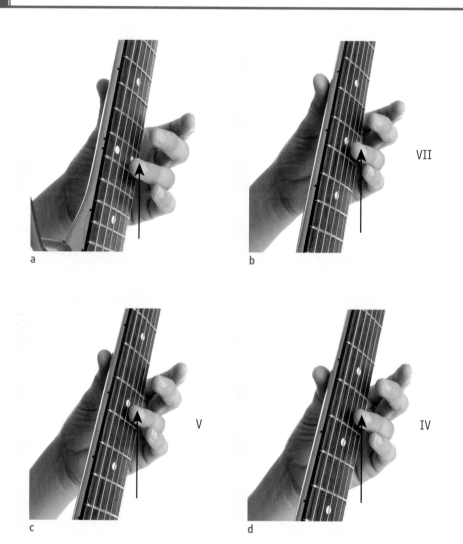

If you touch the string at the 5th fret (c), you'll hear a note two octaves above the open string.

If you touch the string at the 4th fret (d), you'll hear a note two octaves and four semitones above the open string.

Here's how the harmonics look across the fingerboard.

Harmonic on Open String	12th Fret (1 Octave Up)	7th Fret (1 Octave + 7 Chromatic Steps Up)	5th Fret (2 Octaves Up)	4th Fret (2 Octaves + 4 Chromatic Steps Up)
E (1st)	E	B	E	G♯
B (2nd)	B	F♯	B	D♯
G (3rd)	G	D	G	B
D (4th)	D	A	D	F♯
A (5th)	A	E	A	C♯
E (6th)	E	B	E	G♯

Pinch Harmonics

The pinch harmonic is done with a pick and the thumb simultaneously striking or "pinching" the string. It creates a high-frequency harmonic that jumps out. It's used in hard rock, blues, and other guitar styles that involve overdrive and distortion. The harmonic is often hard to hear, so distortion and compression often help bring out harmonic volume.

CHAPTER 16

Purchasing and Maintaining Equipment

With the variety of manufacturers and options available, buying your first guitar can be confusing. That's why it's important to consider several factors before you buy.

Once you own a guitar, you need to know how to take care of it. You can do some of these tasks at home, while others require expert attention.

Because prices vary greatly, there are some factors to consider before making your purchase, including budget. The main consideration, however, should be the guitar's playability and your attraction to its sound.

BRING A KNOWLEDGEABLE FRIEND

Since you look down on the guitar while you're playing, you hear only part of the sound. Bring a friend to the music store with you and have him or her listen to you play. Play in different parts of the room and in different rooms. Also have your friend play and listen to the guitar's sound as you walk around the room. You should be comfortable with the sound from both the player's perspective and the listener's perspective.

TRUST YOUR INSTINCTS

Even though it helps to do as much research as possible, remember that playing a musical instrument is a labor of love. Don't be surprised if you're drawn to an instrument you never thought you'd like. Conversely, don't think you'll grow to love an instrument that's a good deal, but whose sound isn't particularly attractive to you.

BUDGET CONSIDERATIONS

Most high-end guitars are made of solid pieces of high-quality wood, such as maple, rosewood, or ebony. Less expensive models are made of laminated woods that are pressed together. A solid-top guitar (shown here) is usually considered to be a better-sounding instrument and typically sounds better over the years as the wood ages. Expect to spend $400–$500 for a well-crafted model, but let your ears be the final judge. One of my favorite guitars has a solid-wood top and a laminate back and sides, and it cost less than $350.

Many newer guitars are made of laminate wood, making them less expensive to produce. A laminate-top guitar is less likely to warp than a solid-top guitar because of the multiple levels of wood and the lacquer surrounding them. Laminate-top guitars are not as rich in tone as solid-wood guitars made of a single type of wood.

Styles of Acoustic Guitars

Steel-string guitars (see photo) are used in blues, rock, and pop music. They can be used in folk and country music as well. A steel-string guitar is an ideal instrument for songwriting and accompanying singers.

Nylon-string guitars are the only guitars used in classical and flamenco music. They are also used in jazz and Brazilian music. If this is the type of music you intend to play, you want to buy a nylon-string guitar.

Some beginners choose to play a nylon-string guitar over a steel-string guitar because nylon strings are softer to the touch, especially for a beginner still building calluses. The nylon-string neck is also slightly wider than the steel-string neck, which makes classical fingerstyle easier to play.

TIP

If you have very large hands or fingers, you may want to try a nylon-string guitar. Most nylon-string guitars have wider spacing between the strings to accommodate the classical technique (often referred to as the "Segovia Technique" after famed classical guitarist Andrés Segovia), where the junction of the skin and nail is used to pluck the strings.

The electric guitar offers more factors to consider. The type of body construction varies even more than in acoustic guitars, and the electronics and pickups alter the way the strings are heard.

Body Construction

The most common body type for modern electric guitars is the solid body. Les Paul developed the first prototypes of his namesake solid-body guitars in the 1950s. Leo Fender headed up a parallel development of solid-body guitars. These guitars are great for modern applications of rock, country, blues, and pop. They have a present and punchy tone and will not feed back under normal situations.

Some guitars, such as the Gibson Les Paul, are made of several layers of different types of solid wood.

Other guitars, such as the Fender Telecaster, have bodies made of one piece of wood. Solid-body guitars are less susceptible to amplifier feedback. They are generally less expensive than their semi-hollow counterparts.

Semi-hollow guitars, such as the Gibson ES-335, have a solid block of wood running down the middle of the instrument, while the sides are hollow. This design produces a sound that is punchy but still has some acoustic depth.

Pickups

A pickup is a specially designed microphonic device that delivers the sound of the guitar's strings to an amplifier, without most of the incidental noise. The two most common pickups are the single-coil pickup and the humbucker pickup.

A single-coil pickup has a clear, bell-like tone and is great for modern applications of rock, country, blues, and pop. Most of the traditional Fender-style guitars, such as the Telecaster and Stratocaster (see photo), have single-coil pickups.

The humbucker pickup was developed to combat the noise that a single-coil pickup often encounters. The humbucker is essentially two single-coil pickups wound together with wire. The interaction of the two coils magnetically cancels out noise and electronic hum, hence the name *humbucker*. These pickups have a broader sound with more emphasis in the midrange. If you're planning on playing rock, heavy blues, or jazz, this might be the pickup for you.

TIP

Buying Used or Renting

A used guitar can be a great value; many vintage instruments are prized for their tone and collectability. However, a used guitar might cost a lot to repair later.

Renting a guitar may be a viable option if you're not sure how much you want to spend or what kind of guitar you want. But a rental may be hard to play if the store hasn't adjusted the action. If the strings seem to be so high above the neck that it's hard for your fingers to press down, the guitar is considered to have "high action." Ask a salesperson to adjust it before you take it home. As a beginner, it's important for you to play on a guitar that's set up properly so you aren't working harder than necessary.

An electric guitar and an amplifier work as a team to shape the instrument's final sound. The type of amp and the electronic options it offers can drastically change the sound of the guitar and how it functions in any musical genre. The most important factor is whether the electric guitar's sound is being amplified on older vacuum-tube technology or more recent solid-state technology.

TUBE AMPLIFIERS

Tube amplifiers generally sound warmer and feel more touch-sensitive than solid-state amplifiers. However, they also require more maintenance. Tubes will eventually need to be replaced, and you will occasionally need to have a service professional adjust the bias or voltage setting.

SOLID-STATE AMPLIFIERS

Solid-state amplifiers are often more affordable than tube amplifiers and do not require regular maintenance. They are not usually thought to have the same richness in sound as tube amps, but solid-state amps have been improving steadily over the years. Newer models often incorporate modeling technology, which enables them to imitate any number of sounds, replicating older amps and effects. Effects like distortion, reverb, vibrato, chorus, and delay are common in modern amps. However, if they break, they're often hard to fix.

Care for and Maintain Your Strings

Taking care of your strings can prolong their lifespan. By doing so, your strings will be able to retain their tonal clarity and their ability to stay in tune longer.

PROLONG THE LIFE OF YOUR STRINGS

To make your strings last longer, wipe them down with a clean, dry cloth after you finish playing. Doing so prevents sweat and dirt from oxidizing on the strings.

There are other things you can do to prolong the life of your strings. Excessive heat, cold, and humidity can reduce a string's lifespan. Avoid keeping the guitar in the trunk of your car during extreme weather.

KNOW WHEN TO CHANGE YOUR STRINGS

In time, sweat and dirt from your hands will start to tarnish and dull the guitar strings. Eventually, the high-end brilliance and low-end bass frequencies will suffer. The guitar will sound less vibrant and full and will not ring as long.

A guitar with old strings is also harder to tune. The strings become fatigued from the constant pressure of being stretched across the guitar. You may need to retune certain strings constantly. Some strings may seem to be in tune for one chord but out of tune for others. In either situation, you should change your strings.

FAQ

Is there an average lifespan for a guitar string?

Absolutely not. I change my strings every two weeks. My other professional friends can go months. Although strings can physically last for years, you'll notice an improvement in sound quality if you change your strings at least every two to three months.

Change your guitar strings whenever the tone or tuning suffers. Here's how to restring quickly and easily.

Restring a Steel-String Acoustic Guitar

1 Remove the old string. You'll see that one end of the string is held in place by a ball end, which is placed in the hole of the bridge and held in place by a bridge pin. If you can't remove the bridge pin manually, use a string winder, which has a notch that you can use to pry the pin out.

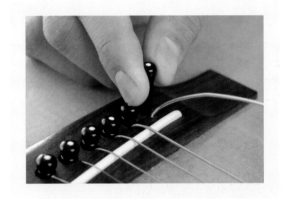

2 After you've removed the bridge pin, place the new string back in the hole. Replace the pin so the groove in the pin faces the nut. The pressure of tuning the string up to pitch will keep the bridge pin in place. Keep light pressure on the pin if it shifts (see photo).

3 Reserve a length of string to wrap around the tuner. Assume that you'll need about 2 inches of string beyond where the string reaches the tuner. Bend that string as a reference point and thread it through the tuner so the string is turned around the top of the tuner.

4 Thread the string through the hole of the tuner.

5 As you hold the string taut with your right hand, slowly wind the tuner so the tension on the string increases (see photo). The first wrap of the string should be above the string length you're holding. After the first wrap is complete, the rest of the windings should be underneath the string length and continue winding downward.

6 The first wrap of the string should be above the original string length (a). Subsequent wraps should be below the original string length and continue downward (b).

a

b

7 While tuning the string up to pitch, you may want to pull on the string at the 12th fret to let it stretch. Doing so stops the string from stretching out while you play. It also prevents tangled windings while you turn the tuners.

NOTE: Remember to keep your string windings neat as you restring your guitar. A crooked string winding will resettle while you play, throwing your string out of tune.

Restring a Nylon-String Acoustic Guitar

Even more so than with steel strings, you have to stretch out nylon strings before you start playing.

BALL-END STRINGS
Some nylon-string guitars use strings that have ball ends similar to steel strings. In those cases, simply place one end of the string through the bridge, then wind the other end through the tuner as described in the earlier section "Restring a Steel-String Acoustic Guitar."

SPECIAL TIES
Classical and flamenco nylon-string guitars require a special tie to fasten the string. Once you place the string through the tailpiece, you bring it back up and wrap it around the top of the string. Then you wrap the remaining string length around the original length toward the bottom of the bridge.

Restring an Electric Guitar

Restringing an electric guitar is similar to restringing an acoustic guitar, but you thread the ball end of the string through a metal bridge piece. Some guitars, such as the Fender Telecaster (a) and Stratocaster, allow the strings to pass through the bridge saddle all the way through the body (b).

a

b

Other guitars, such as the Gibson Les Paul, have a tailpiece on the top of the guitar where the string starts.

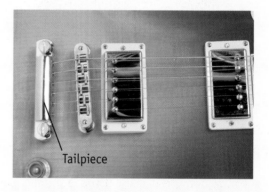

Tailpiece

Other guitars have a moveable bridge where you can lower the pitch of the strings by depressing a movable arm known as a *tremolo bar*.

The other end of the string is fastened to the tuner as described in the earlier section, "Restring a Steel-String Acoustic Guitar."

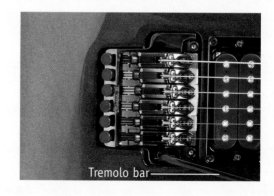

Tremolo bar

It's important to have your guitar's truss rod set up correctly so that the guitar is easy to play and free from buzzing.

WHAT IS THE TRUSS ROD?

Steel-string acoustic and electric guitars have a steel rod inside the neck called a truss rod. The truss rod controls how much the neck bends. The neck must have a slight bend or the strings will buzz when pressed down. Nylon-string guitars and older or less expensive steel-string guitars do not have a truss rod.

The end of the truss rod is found either at the top of the headstock underneath a cover (a) or simply within a hole (b), or where the neck meets the body inside the guitar. You adjust the truss rod by using a hex wrench. It needs to be adjusted seasonally as weather and humidity levels change.

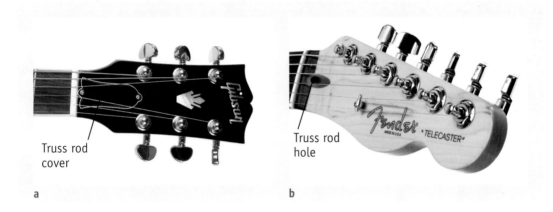

Truss rod
cover

Truss rod
hole

a   b

LET A PRO FIX THE TRUSS ROD FOR NOW

If the neck of your guitar is too flat, the strings will buzz, especially if played with a lot of dynamics. However, you don't want the guitar strings so high that it's uncomfortable or difficult for your fingers to push the strings down, especially if you're playing barre chords or chords that involve the pinky of your fretting hand. The initial adjustments should be made by a guitar repair professional to ensure that there are no other issues, and so that you have to perform only simple maintenance tasks at home, but here's how to do it when you know your way around the guitar a bit better.

If the strings are buzzing excessively, especially on the first six frets, the truss rod may be too tight. Loosen it by turning the truss rod wrench counterclockwise no more than an eighth of a turn each time. If the strings are too high, especially around the twelfth fret, the truss rod may be too loose. Tighten it by turning the truss rod wrench clockwise, again no more than an eighth of a turn each time.

Don't tighten the truss rod too hard; excessive pressure could cause it to break, and replacing a truss rod is expensive. Let the guitar sit overnight before making another adjustment; it may take a while for the truss rod adjustment to affect the action. If the problem doesn't resolve itself, take the guitar to a repair professional.

Adjust Intonation on an Electric Guitar

If your electric guitar doesn't seem to be in tune consistently across the neck (fretting sharp or flat), it may be intonated improperly. Here's an easy way to adjust the intonation with just an electronic tuner and a screwdriver.

TUNE THE OPEN STRINGS FIRST

Before you intonate your guitar, start with a fresh set of strings. You may have to re-intonate the guitar if you use a different gauge of strings or change the height of the bridge.

For each string, hit the open string and use your electronic tuner to tune it. (See the section "Tuning with an Electronic Tuner" in Chapter 3.)

TUNE THE 12TH FRET OF THE SAME STRING

After tuning the open string, play the 12th fret, which is the same note, one octave up.

- If the 12th fret note is exactly the same according to your tuner, that string is properly intonated.

- If the note on the 12th fret is flatter (lower in pitch) than the open string, use a screwdriver to turn the screw on the saddle on which the string rests so that it moves forward. Doing so raises the pitch of the 12th note relative to the open string.

- If the note on the 12th fret is sharper (higher in pitch) than the open string, use the screwdriver to turn the screw on the saddle on which the string rests so that it moves backward. Doing so lowers the pitch of the 12th note relative to the open string.

After each screwdriver adjustment, retune the open string using the tuner, and then recheck the 12th fret note. Repeat this process until both notes are in tune.

D ry air can dry out your guitar, causing damage to its structure and finish. Luckily, it's easy to care for the instrument with a few humidification tips.

KEEP YOUR GUITAR FROM DRYING OUT

When cold temperatures set in, it's easy for the wood in your guitar to dry out. Low humidity can cause cracking to both the finish and the wood.

If you don't return your guitar to its case after playing, you should use a room humidifier. Even better is placing the guitar in its case with a small guitar humidifier in the soundhole. The humidifier will release a small amount of water into the soundhole in a controlled manner.

Place guitar humidifier here

KNOW WHEN TO CALL IN A PRO

Here are some procedures you should let a professional handle.

Go to a Professional for These Jobs	
Problem	**What's Wrong**
The body underneath the bridge is swollen and curved, pushing the strings away from the fingerboard.	Excessive dryness has caused the wood to warp.
The first several frets are too high to play.	The nut and/or action may need to be adjusted.
The volume/tone controls make a scratchy noise through the amp when moved.	The control pots are dirty and need to be cleaned.
The strings rattle and fret out when played.	The action needs to be adjusted.
The bridge on your tremolo bridge keeps rising when you try to tune the guitar.	There is not enough tension holding the bridge in place, and it needs to be adjusted.

CHAPTER 17

Electric Guitar Sounds

While an electric guitar has the same tuning and fingerboard layout as an acoustic guitar, its sound can be manipulated in ways an acoustic guitar's can't. With the advent of digital technology, many modern amps can mimic a variety of vintage amps and effects. You can select a sound that resembles a small tube amp, a medium-sized solid-state amp, or a 100-watt amp-and-speaker combination. Some amps can also add the sounds of delays, reverbs, choruses, and other pedal processors that are often purchased separately. This chapter looks at controls on the guitar, the amplifier, and effect processing.

The volume control, tone control, and pickup selectors on your guitar enable you to change the sound leaving the guitar before it gets to the amplifier.

Volume control

Volume controls

Tone controls

The **volume control** affects the volume output that leaves the guitar. Some guitars, such as the Fender Stratocaster (pictured here) and Telecaster, have one master output. You have only one knob to turn, even if you're using more than one pickup at a time.

NOTE: In many guitars, as you turn the volume down, you may hear an incidental drop in the guitar's treble frequencies. One guitar that doesn't have this problem is the Telecaster, which has an extra capacitor in the wiring.

Other guitars, such as the Les Paul and the Gibson SG (pictured here), have a control assigned to each pickup.

Tone control affects the treble or high-end content of the guitar's tone. When the tone control is turned all the way up, the guitar's sound is unaltered. As you turn the knob, the sound becomes darker and less trebly. Many guitarists who play jazz, blues, or ballads do this to get a warmer, more hornlike sound.

As with the volume control, your guitar may have more than one tone control. Pictured here are the tone controls on the ES-335. The Stratocaster is an interesting variation because it has a tone control for each pickup except the rear pickup. The tone is then controlled by the treble control on an amplifier.

Controls on Your Amplifier

The amplifier controls are the last factors you can control before an electric guitar's sound hits your ears. Let's investigate how the amplifier's volume, tone, reverb, and other controls affect the guitar's sound.

Volume Controls

Some traditional amps, such as the Fender Twin amp, have only one master volume control that makes the amplifier's volume louder or softer.

Newer amps may have a master volume control, plus a secondary overdrive, distortion, or gain control to create a distorted sound. First, you use the overdrive/gain knob to control how much distortion you want. Then you slowly turn the master volume control up until you reach the desired playing volume.

More advanced amplifiers might have two sets of volume controls: one for a traditional clean, undistorted sound and one for overdriven sounds. See the section "Effect Pedals" later in this chapter for more on overdrive.

Gain control Volume control

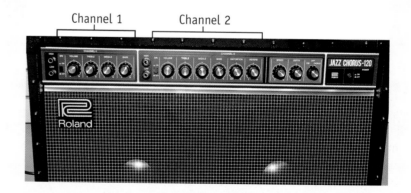

Channel 1   Channel 2

Tone, Reverb, and Tremolo Controls

Tone control on an amplifier typically consists of treble, midrange (or "mid"), and bass controls. Some amplifiers also have a presence knob or a bright switch, which allows for even brighter frequency control than a traditional treble control.

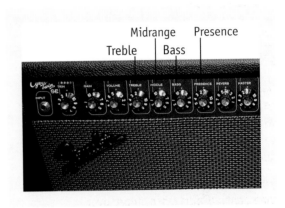
Treble   Midrange   Bass   Presence

Your amp may have a reverb control, which simulates a cavernous sound, as if you were playing in a large amphitheater or concert hall.

Reverb knob

Another common feature is a set of controls for tremolo, which allows for an undulating or wobbling change of the guitar's intensity. The controls are usually labeled "intensity" (how strong the tremolo's pulse is) and "speed" (how fast the pulse moves). Reverb and tremolo used together was a common staple of '50s and '60s surf music. Classic tremolo songs include Tommy James and the Shondells' "Crimson and Clover," Creedence Clearwater Revival's "Born on the Bayou," and the Smiths' "How Soon Is Now?"

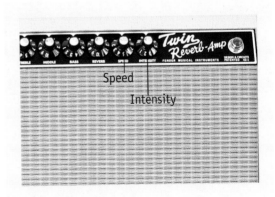
Speed   Intensity

Effect Pedals

By using effect pedals, you can alter the sound of your guitar and add electronic color, enhancing the possibilities of what the guitar alone can do.

The most common pedal for many players involves overdrive, distortion, or fuzz. All of these effects involve changing the gain structure of the electric guitar's sound.

Overdrive, Distortion, and Fuzz

OVERDRIVE

Overdrive is the most subtle of the effects. It simulates the sound of a tube amplifier when it's turned louder. It allows you to have a more sustained sound, plus a crunchier edge—think of Stevie Ray Vaughan. An overdrive pedal is a convenient way to switch between sounds quickly by turning the pedal on and off between overdriven and clean sounds.

DISTORTION

Distortion is a harder, dirtier, more intense sound than overdrive, and even further removed from the original electric guitar tone. There is more sustain and higher levels of gain are produced. Distortion is used in hard rock, heavy metal, punk, and alternative music. Think of ZZ Top's or Queen's heavy-distortion songs.

FUZZ

Fuzz is a more extreme version of distortion. A fuzz pedal is fatter and less subtle than either overdrive or distortion. Fuzz also adds a lot of extra noise to the guitar's sound, so players must mute the strings not played or they may start feeding back. Many rock icons—think Jimi Hendrix, Jeff Beck, and Jack White—favored these pedals.

Other Pedals

A **delay pedal** allows one or more echoes to be heard after you play a note. A short delay is called a *slapback.* Many early rock and rockabilly records use slapback echoes on guitar and vocals to create a punchy echo. Longer echoes can be used to create intertwining sounds that give the illusion of multiple guitar players. Think of the echo textures of the Police's Andy Summers or U2's the Edge.

A **reverb pedal** is similar to a delay pedal but uses many delayed signals to approximate the sound of the guitar echoing in a large concert hall or theater, as in the outro of "Over the Hills and Far Away" by Led Zeppelin. This pedal can also be used in conjunction with amps that do not have their own reverb controls.

A **volume pedal** does the same thing as the volume knob on your guitar, but leaves both of your hands free to play the guitar because your foot controls the volume. The pedal is based on a rocker mechanism that turns a control. Pressing the pedal with your heel turns the guitar's volume completely off. Pressing with your toe turns the guitar's volume fully on. You can use the volume pedal to control the output of the guitar by moving it up and down while you play. If you leave the pedal in the down position (sound completely off) and then hit a string, the guitar sounds like a bowed violin when you press your toe on the pedal.

A **wah-wah (or "wah") pedal** looks like a volume pedal, but the control changes a boost in tone. As you move your foot from heel to toe over the rocker mechanism, the sound of the guitar swells from a bassier to a more trebly tone, imitating the sound of a human voice.

Chord Charts

Here's a compilation of many of the chords taught in this book. As you get more adept at your playing, you can use this appendix as a quick, at-a-glance reference for many of the common chords you will encounter. For information about how to read a chord chart, see Chapter 5.

Major and Minor Chords

OPEN

A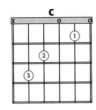
C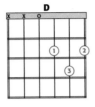
D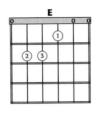
E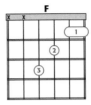
F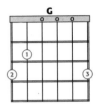
G

Am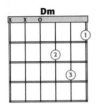
Dm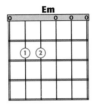
Em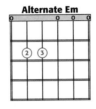
Alternate Em

A (open row)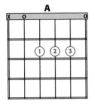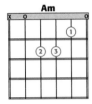

SEVENTH

A7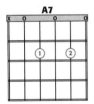
B7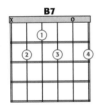
C7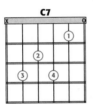
D7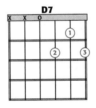
E7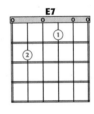
G7

Am7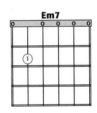
Em7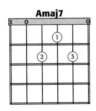
Amaj7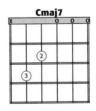
Cmaj7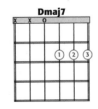
Dmaj7
Fmaj7

241

E-Shaped Barre Chords

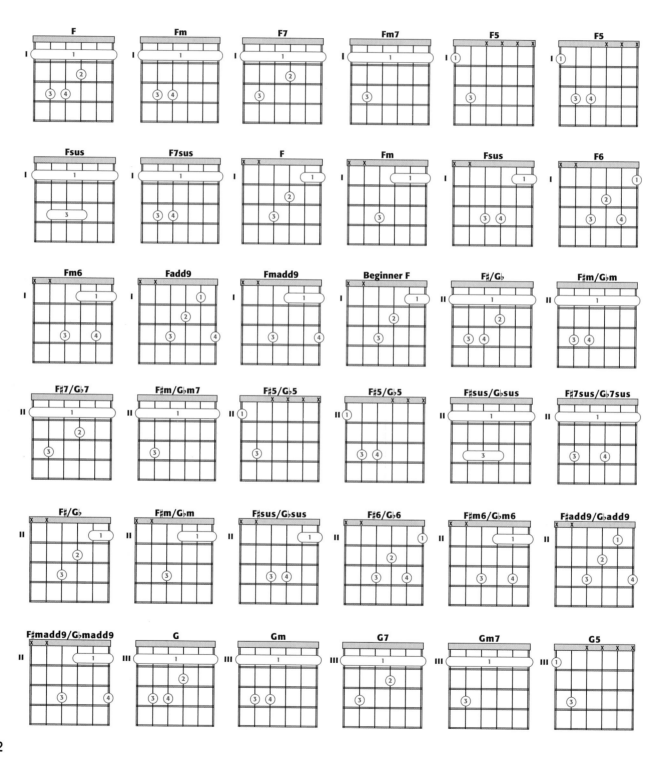

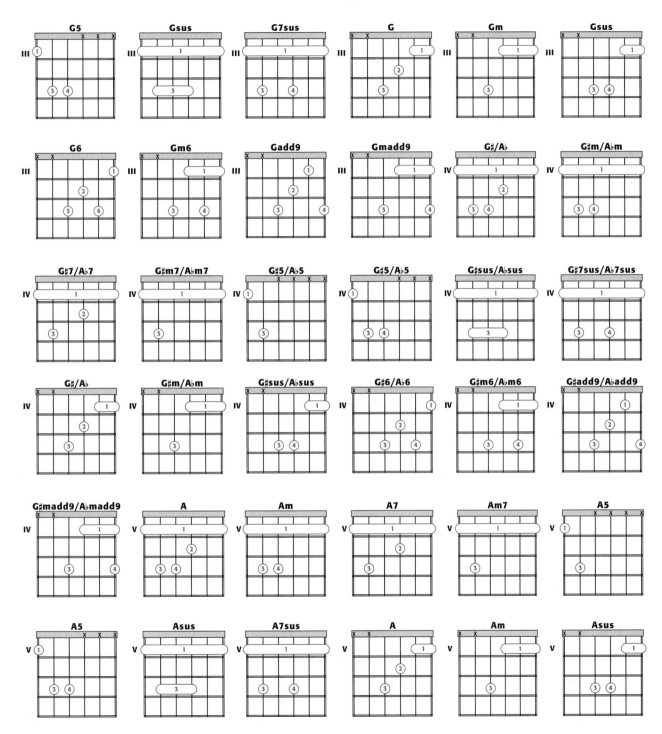

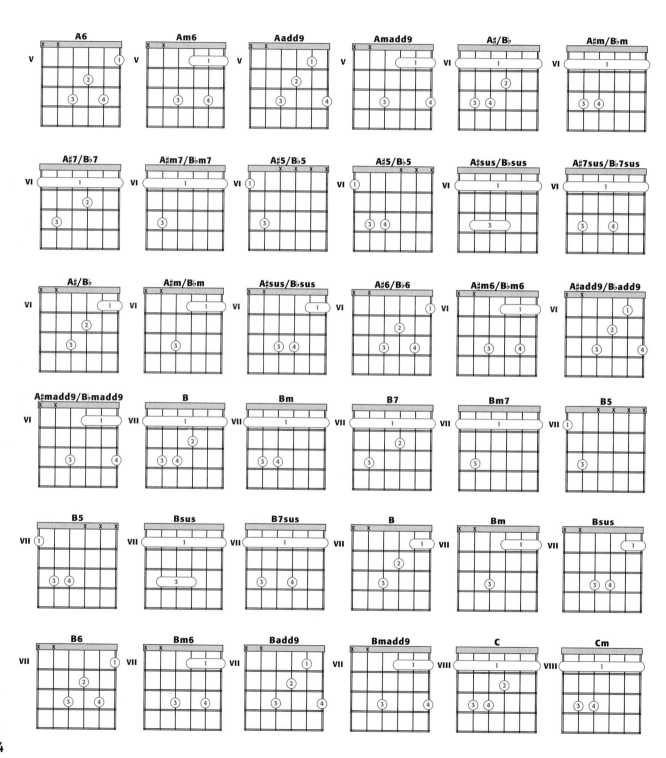

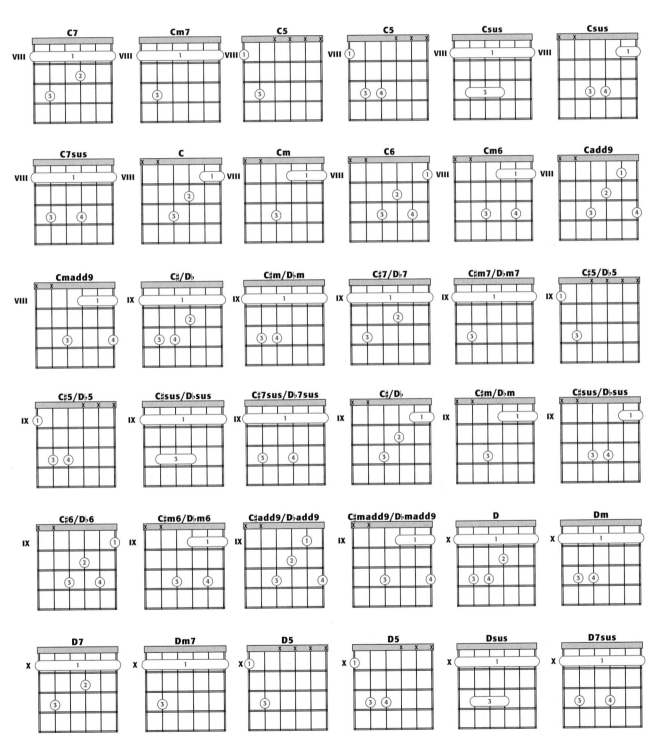

245

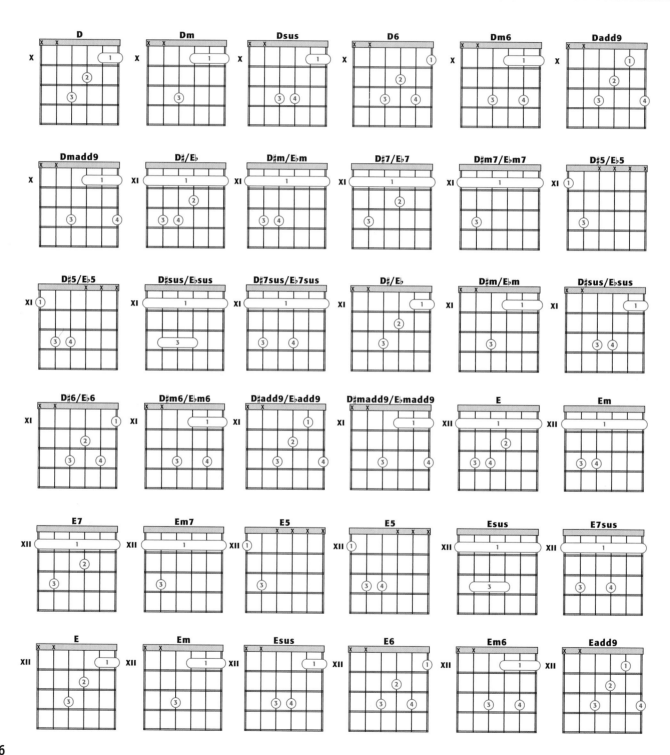

A-Shaped Barre Chords

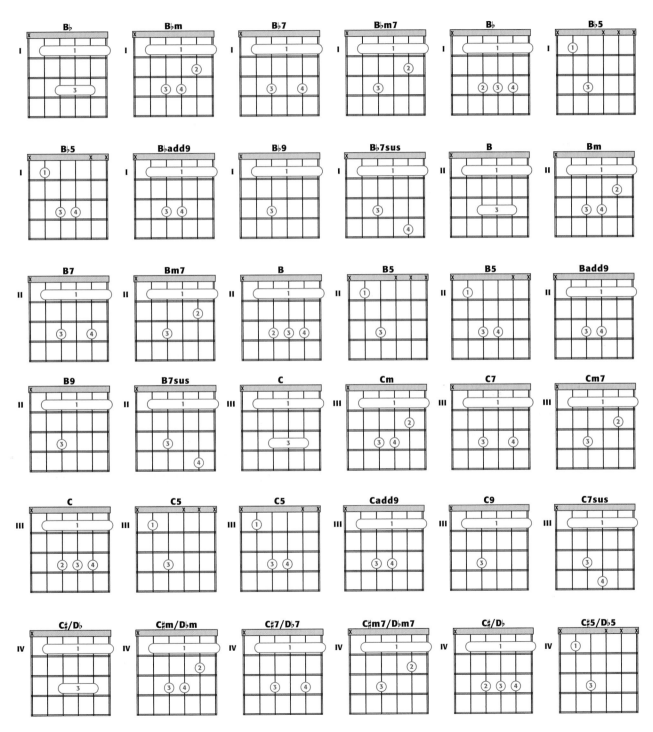

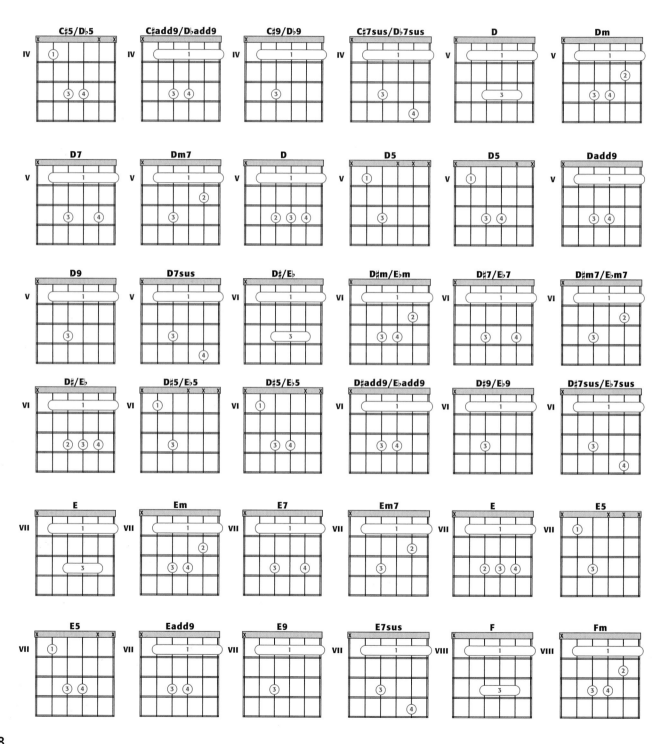

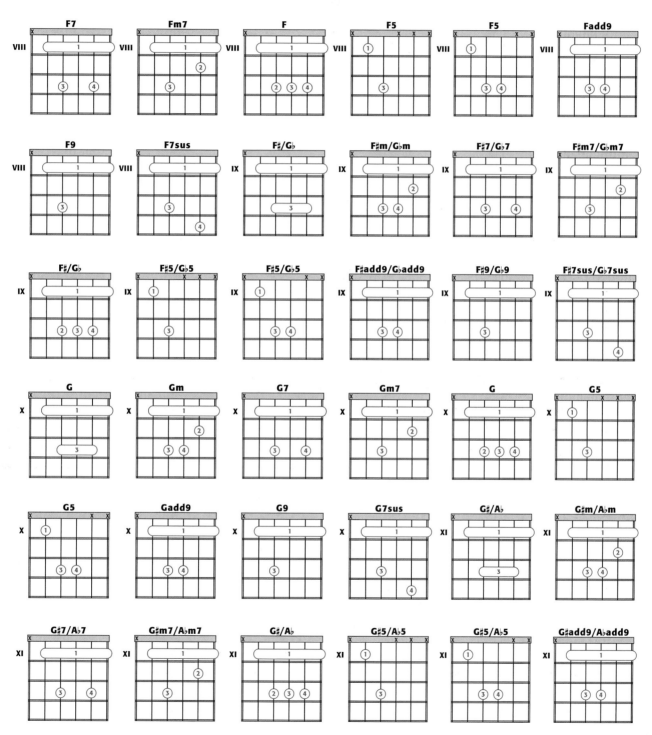

A-Shaped Barre Chords *(continued)*

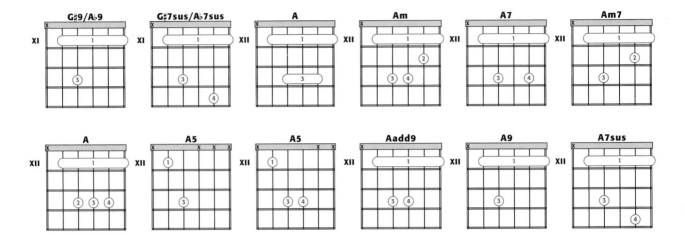

Scales

This appendix includes several basic scales that you can use while warming up and practicing. Playing scales isn't as much fun as playing songs, but scales are important for dexterity and musical knowledge, and understanding and practicing them will enable you to master more complex and accomplished pieces.

Open scales are scale formations for which you use open strings whenever possible, as opposed to the same pitches in fretted positions. Sometimes they are preferable because of the bright, ringy sounds of the open strings.

Movable scales don't use open strings, but have shapes that can move as units up and down the neck. For example, the scale pattern for A minor pentatonic looks exactly like the pattern for B minor pentatonic in terms of relative finger movements except that the A minor pentatonic starts on the 5th fret of the E (6th) string, where as the B minor pentatonic starts on the 7th fret. Movable scales are sometimes preferable because every note can be played with vibrato, and learning one pattern allows you to play it any key.

Major Open Scales

A MAJOR

C MAJOR

D MAJOR

E MAJOR

G MAJOR

Major Movable Scales

A MAJOR MOVABLE

C MAJOR MOVABLE

D MAJOR MOVABLE

E MAJOR MOVABLE

G MAJOR MOVABLE

Minor Open Scales

F♯ MINOR

A MINOR

B MINOR

B C# D E F# G A B C# D E F# G A B

C# MINOR

C# D# E F# G# A B C# D# E F# G# A B C#

E MINOR

E F# G A B C D E F# G A B C D E

Minor Movable Scales

F# MINOR MOVABLE

F# G# A B C# D E F# G# A B C# D E F#

A MINOR MOVABLE

A B C D E F G A B C D E F G A

B MINOR MOVABLE

B C# D E F# G A B C# D E F# G A B

C# MINOR MOVABLE

C# D# E F# G# A B C# D# E F# G# A B C#

E MINOR MOVABLE

Major Pentatonic Open Scales

A MAJOR PENTATONIC

C MAJOR PENTATONIC

D MAJOR PENTATONIC

E MAJOR PENTATONIC

G MAJOR PENTATONIC

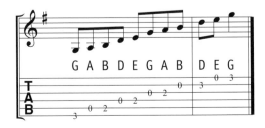

Major Pentatonic Movable Scales

A MAJOR PENTATONIC MOVABLE

C MAJOR PENTATONIC MOVABLE

D MAJOR PENTATONIC MOVABLE

E MAJOR PENTATONIC MOVABLE

G MAJOR PENTATONIC MOVABLE

Minor Pentatonic Open Scales

F# MINOR PENTATONIC

A MINOR PENTATONIC

256

B MINOR PENTATONIC

C# MINOR PENTATONIC

E MINOR PENTATONIC

Minor Pentatonic Movable Scales

F# MINOR PENTATONIC MOVABLE

A MINOR PENTATONIC MOVABLE

B MINOR PENTATONIC MOVABLE

C# MINOR PENTATONIC MOVABLE

E MINOR PENTATONIC MOVABLE

Blues Scales

A BLUES

C BLUES

D BLUES

E BLUES

G BLUES

Index

Numbers

1st string. *See* High E string
2nd string. *See* B string
3/4 time, 90, 177
3rd string. *See* G string
4/4 time, 85–89, 177
4th string. *See* D string
5th string. *See* A string
6th string. *See* Low E string

A

A7 chord, 44, 107, 129
A blues scale, 189, 192, 258
accidentals, 178
A chord, 49, 107, 129
acoustic guitar
    buying, 221–222
    maintenance for, 226–229,
      231, 233
    parts of, 7, 9–14, 221–222, 231
    restringing, 227–229
alternate bass run patterns, 151–154
Am7 chord, 51, 107
A major (F♯ minor) key, 179
A major movable scale, 180, 252
A major pentatonic movable scale, 255
A major pentatonic scale, 190, 254
A major scale, 171, 180, 251
Am chord, 50, 107, 129
A minor movable scale, 172, 253
A minor pentatonic movable scale, 256
A minor pentatonic scale, 191, 255, 257
A minor scale, 172, 252
amplifier, 225, 236–237
Amsus2 chord, 137
Amsus4 chord, 138
anchoring, 73
arpeggios, 73–76, 98, 126–132
A-shaped barre chords, 120–124,
    247–250

A string (5th string)
    on chord chart, 41
    notes on, 168–169
    in tablature, 97
    tuning, 24, 25, 27
Asus2 chord, 136
Asus4 chord, 136

B

B♭ major (G minor) key, 179, 181, 182
B♭ major movable scale, 182
B♭ major scale, 171, 182
B5 power chord, 123
B7 barre chord, 121–122
B7 chord, 52, 107, 129
bar, 85
barre chords. *See also specific chords*
    A-shaped, 120–124, 247–250
    E-shaped, 109–119, 242–246
bass control, on amplifier, 237
bass runs
    alternate patterns for, 151–154
    described, 146
    playing, 146–147
    single-note patterns for, 148–151
    walking patterns for, 155–165
B barre chord, 121–122
blue note, 186, 188, 189
blues
    pickups for, 224
    pinch harmonics for, 219
    seventh chords for, 94
    string bending for, 215
    tone controls for, 235
    type of strings for, 15, 222
    vertical vibrato for, 214
blues scales
    described, 186
    list of, 258
    playing, 187–189
    solos using, 192, 194, 196,
      199, 200

Bm7 barre chord, 121–122
Bm barre chord, 120–121
Bm chord, arpeggios on, 130
B minor (D major) key, 179, 180
B minor movable scale, 172, 253
B minor pentatonic movable scale, 256
B minor pentatonic scale, 256
B minor scale, 172, 253
body
    of acoustic guitar, 7, 221
    described, 12–13
    of electric guitar, 8, 223
bridge, 7, 14. *See also* tremolo bar
B string (2nd string)
    on chord chart, 41
    notes on, 167, 169
    in tablature, 97
    tuning, 24, 26, 27

C

C♯ minor (E major) key, 179, 180
C♯ minor movable scale, 173, 253
C♯ minor pentatonic movable scale, 256
C♯ minor pentatonic scale, 256
C♯ minor scale, 173, 253
C7 chord, 54, 107, 130
capo, 104–108
C blues scale, 188, 194, 258
C chord, 53, 107, 130
chord charts, 41, 241–249
chords. *See also specific chords*
    barre chords. *See* barre chords
    described, 40
    list of, 241–249
    major chords, 92–93, 241
    minor chords, 93, 241
    moved up by using a capo,
      104–108
    moving between, 62–68
    ninth chords, 135
    open chords, 42–45, 48–60

chords *(continued)*

    seventh chords, 94, 95, 96

    in tablature, 98

chromatic scale

    capo affecting, 104–105

    described, 21, 92, 167

    playing, 168–170

chromatic tuner, 21–24

classical guitar music, 15, 30, 222

classical vibrato, 213

C major key, 179

C major movable scale, 180, 252

C major pentatonic movable scale, 255

C major pentatonic scale, 187, 192, 254

C major scale, 171, 180, 251

C minor (E♭ major) key, 179, 181, 183

C minor pentatonic scale, 187, 193, 257

country music, 15, 215, 222, 224

Csus2 chord, 139

D

D7 chord, 55, 131

D7sus4 chord, 140

D blues scale, 196, 258

D chord, 42–43, 126–128, 130

delay pedal, 239

distortion effect, 238

Dmadd2 chord, 141

D major (B minor) key, 179, 180

D major movable scale, 180, 252

D major pentatonic movable scale, 255

D major pentatonic scale, 194, 254

D major scale, 171, 180, 251

Dm chord, 56, 131

D minor (F major) key, 179, 181, 182

D minor pentatonic scale, 195, 257

dominant seventh chords, 94

dotted notes, 176

D string (4th string)

    on chord chart, 41

    notes on, 168–169

in tablature, 97

    tuning, 24, 26, 27

Dsus2 chord, 133–134, 139

Dsus4 chord, 134, 140

E

E♭ major (C minor) key, 179, 181, 183

E♭ major movable scale, 182

E♭ major scale, 171, 182

E7 chord, 58, 107, 131

E7sus4 chord, 142

E blues scale, 199, 258

E chord, 57, 107, 131

effect pedals, 238–239

eighth notes, 175

electric guitar

    amplifier for, 225, 236–237

    buying, 223–224

    effect pedals for, 238–239

    intonation, adjusting, 232

    maintenance for, 226, 230–233

    parts of, 8–14, 16–18, 223–224, 231

    restringing, 230

    sitting position for, 31

electronic chromatic tuner, 21–24

Em7 chord, 59, 107

E major (C♯ minor) key, 179, 180

E major movable scale, 180, 252

E major pentatonic movable scale, 255

E major pentatonic scale, 197, 254

E major scale, 170–171, 180, 251

Em chord, 58–59, 107, 132

E minor (G major) key, 179, 181

E minor movable scale, 173, 254

E minor pentatonic movable scale, 257

E minor pentatonic scale, 198, 256, 257

E minor scale, 173, 253

Emsus2 chord, 143

Emsus4 chord, 143

end pin, 13

enharmonic notes, 21, 92, 167

E-shaped barre chords, 109–119, 242–246

E strings. *See* High E string; Low E string

Esus4 chord, 142

Every Good Boy Does Fine (mnemonic), 174

F

F♯5 power chord, 117–118

F♯7 barre chord, 116

F♯ barre chord, 116

F♯m7 barre chord, 118

F♯m barre chord, 117

F♯ minor (A major) key, 179

F♯ minor movable scale, 173, 253

F♯ minor pentatonic movable scale, 256

F♯ minor pentatonic scale, 255

F♯ minor scale, 173, 252

F♭ minor (A major) key, 178, 179

F5 power chord, 115

F7 barre chord, 114

FACE (mnemonic), 174

F barre chord, 111–113

F chord, arpeggios on, 132

Fender Stratocaster guitar

    bridge, 14

    pickups, 224

    restringing, 230

    tone controls, 235

    volume controls, 235

Fender Telecaster guitar

    body, 12, 223

    bridge, 14

    pickups, 224

    restringing, 230

    tone controls, 18

    volume controls, 17, 235

Fender Twin amp, 236

fingerboard, 7, 8, 10

fingerboard, map of, 169

John Wiley & Sons, Inc. End-User License Agreement

READ THIS. You should carefully read these terms and conditions before opening the software packet(s) included with this book "Book". This is a license agreement "Agreement" between you and John Wiley & Sons, Inc. "Wiley". By opening the accompanying software packet(s), you acknowledge that you have read and accept the following terms and conditions. If you do not agree and do not want to be bound by such terms and conditions, promptly return the Book and the unopened software packet(s) to the place you obtained them for a full refund.

1. **License Grant.** Wiley grants to you (either an individual or entity) a nonexclusive license to use one copy of the enclosed software program(s) (collectively, the "Software") solely for your own personal or business purposes on a single computer (whether a standard computer or a workstation component of a multi-user network). The Software is in use on a computer when it is loaded into temporary memory (RAM) or installed into permanent memory (hard disk, CD-ROM, or other storage device). Wiley reserves all rights not expressly granted herein.

2. **Ownership.** Wiley is the owner of all right, title, and interest, including copyright, in and to the compilation of the Software recorded on the physical packet included with this Book "Software Media". Copyright to the individual programs recorded on the Software Media is owned by the author or other authorized copyright owner of each program. Ownership of the Software and all proprietary rights relating thereto remain with Wiley and its licensers.

3. **Restrictions on Use and Transfer.**

   (a) You may only (i) make one copy of the Software for backup or archival purposes, or (ii) transfer the Software to a single hard disk, provided that you keep the original for backup or archival purposes. You may not (i) rent or lease the Software, (ii) copy or reproduce the Software through a LAN or other network system or through any computer subscriber system or bulletin-board system, or (iii) modify, adapt, or create derivative works based on the Software.

   (b) You may not reverse engineer, decompile, or disassemble the Software. You may transfer the Software and user documentation on a permanent basis, provided that the transferee agrees to accept the terms and conditions of this Agreement and you retain no copies. If the Software is an update or has been updated, any transfer must include the most recent update and all prior versions.

4. **Restrictions on Use of Individual Programs.** You must follow the individual requirements and restrictions detailed for each individual program on the Software Media. These limitations are also contained in the individual license agreements recorded on the Software Media. These limitations may include a requirement that after using the program for a specified period of time, the user must pay a registration fee or discontinue use. By opening the Software packet(s), you agree to abide by the licenses and restrictions for these individual programs that are detailed on the Software Media. None of the material on this Software Media or listed in this Book may ever be redistributed, in original or modified form, for commercial purposes.

5. **Limited Warranty.**

   (a) Wiley warrants that the Software and Software Media are free from defects in materials and workmanship under normal use for a period of sixty (60) days from the date of purchase of this Book. If Wiley receives notification within the warranty period of defects in materials or workmanship, Wiley will replace the defective Software Media.

   (b) WILEY AND THE AUTHOR(S) OF THE BOOK DISCLAIM ALL OTHER WARRANTIES, EXPRESS OR IMPLIED, INCLUDING WITHOUT LIMITATION IMPLIED WARRANTIES OF MERCHANTABILITY AND FITNESS FOR A PARTICULAR PURPOSE, WITH RESPECT TO THE SOFTWARE, THE PROGRAMS, THE SOURCE CODE CONTAINED THEREIN, AND/OR THE TECHNIQUES DESCRIBED IN THIS BOOK. WILEY DOES NOT WARRANT THAT THE FUNCTIONS CONTAINED IN THE SOFTWARE WILL MEET YOUR REQUIREMENTS OR THAT THE OPERATION OF THE SOFTWARE WILL BE ERROR FREE.

   (c) This limited warranty gives you specific legal rights, and you may have other rights that vary from jurisdiction to jurisdiction.

6. **Remedies.**

   (a) Wiley's entire liability and your exclusive remedy for defects in materials and workmanship shall be limited to replacement of the Software Media, which may be returned to Wiley with a copy of your receipt at the following address: Software Media Fulfillment Department, Attn.: *Teach Yourself VISUALLY Guitar, 2nd Edition,* John Wiley & Sons, Inc., 10475 Crosspoint Blvd., Indianapolis, IN 46256, or call 1-877-762-2974. Please allow four to six weeks for delivery. This Limited Warranty is void if failure of the Software Media has resulted from accident, abuse, or misapplication. Any replacement Software Media will be warranted for the remainder of the original warranty period or thirty (30) days, whichever is longer.

   (b) In no event shall Wiley or the author be liable for any damages whatsoever (including without limitation damages for loss of business profits, business interruption, loss of business information, or any other pecuniary loss) arising from the use of or inability to use the Book or the Software, even if Wiley has been advised of the possibility of such damages.

   (c) Because some jurisdictions do not allow the exclusion or limitation of liability for consequential or incidental damages, the above limitation or exclusion may not apply to you.

7. **U.S. Government Restricted Rights.** Use, duplication, or disclosure of the Software for or on behalf of the United States of America, its agencies and/or instrumentalities "U.S. Government" is subject to restrictions as stated in paragraph (c)(1)(ii) of the Rights in Technical Data and Computer Software clause of DFARS 252.227-7013, or subparagraphs (c) (1) and (2) of the Commercial Computer Software - Restricted Rights clause at FAR 52.227-19, and in similar clauses in the NASA FAR supplement, as applicable.

8. **General.** This Agreement constitutes the entire understanding of the parties and revokes and supersedes all prior agreements, oral or written, between them and may not be modified or amended except in a writing signed by both parties hereto that specifically refers to this Agreement. This Agreement shall take precedence over any other documents that may be in conflict herewith. If any one or more provisions contained in this Agreement are held by any court or tribunal to be invalid, illegal, or otherwise unenforceable, each and every other provision shall remain in full force and effect.